For drawings of
2500 H.P. General Purpose
Locomotive GP 35,
see pages 148-149

1. Engine - EMD Mo[...]
2. Main Generator an[...]
3. Generator Blower [...]
4. Auxiliary Generate[...]
5. Control Cabinet
6. Air Compressor
7. Traction Motor Blower
8. Engineer's Control
9. Fuel Pump
10. Engine Exhaust Stack
11. Air Brake Valve
12. Cab Heater
13. Sliding Seat
14. Hand Brake
15. Sand Box Filler
16. Lube Oil Filler
17. Lube Oil Cooler
18. Engine Water Tank
19. Fuel Pressure Filter
20. Load Regulator
21. 48 Inch Fan and Motor
22. Radiator
23. Horns
24. Exhaust Manifold
25. Sand Box
26. Fuel Filler
27. Headlight - Twin Sealed Beam
28. Batteries
29. Fuel Tank - 2600 Gallons
30. Main Air Reservoir
31. Air Intake And Shutters

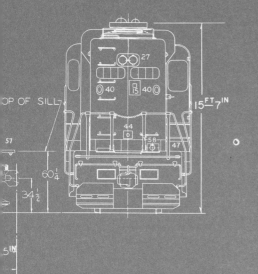

2250 HP ROAD LOCOMOTIVE
MODEL GP30

32. Emergency Fuel Cutoff
33. Engine Room Air Intake
34. Fuel Tank Gauge
35. Trap Door
36. Lube Oil Filter
37. Dual Fuel Filter
38. Engine Air Filter Unit
39. Automatic Drain Valve - No. 1 Reservoir
40. Classification Lights
41. Inertial Air Separator
42. Dust Evacuating Blower
43. Number Box
44. Platform Light
45. Fuel Suction Filter
46. Collision Post
47. Traction Motor Air Duct
48. 36 Inch Fan and Motor
49. Speed Recorder
50. Fire Extinguisher
51. Engine Water Filler
52. Dynamic Brake
53. Signal Light
54. Dynamic Brake Fan
55. Toilet
56. Third Cab Seat
57. Multiple Unit End Arrangement
58. Multiple Unit Receptacle

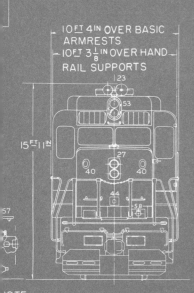

NOTE
LOCO. HEIGHT TOLERANCE   = ± 1 1/2"
LOCO. WIDTH TOLERANCE   = ± 1/2"
TRUCK LATERAL AT BOLSTERS = ± 2 1/4" NOM.

LOCOMOTIVE IS SHOWN INCLUDING FULL
SUPPLIES AND IN NEW CONDITION
STANDING STILL ON LEVEL AND TANGENT
TRACK.

DIESELS WEST!

•

For more than a century, the men and
women of the Burlington have established
and maintained a tradition of excellence.
To all of them—yesterday, today, and
tomorrow—DIESELS WEST! is dedicated.

•

the Evolution of Powe

DIESELS WEST!

by David P. Morgan

on the Burlington

CONTENTS

introduction

David Morgan's DIESELS WEST! illustrates an inspiring fact: Progress is a continuous, never-ending process.

Of course, this is not true of the Burlington alone. However, a careful examination of this railroad at this time provides dramatic evidence of the continuing nature of progress. The Burlington's new diesel locomotives (GP30 and GP35), for example, are bringing added efficiency to Burlington freight operations, just as the original freight diesels of 1944 did when they supplanted steam power. Other innovations demonstrate this principle of continuing progress: cars on roller bearings that will improve performance and (we hope) make us forget the word "hotbox" . . . refrigerator cars, with mechanical cooling and polyurethane foam insulation, that can carry frozen foods from coast to coast without pausing once at an icing dock . . . long tri-level flat cars that can carry 12 standard or 15 compact automobiles . . . and many others.

This drama of railroad renaissance is nationwide and industry-wide. And, to men of the Burlington, this railroad's role in the pageant is something special. Each of us can say, as he would say at Plymouth Rock or Independence Hall, "It all started right here." And "right here," to Burlington men, is the specific point in history at which this railroad turned its attention from our magnificent steam engines to the early diesels. This point is marked by the Pioneer Zephyr.

The Pioneer Zephyr—Burlington 9900—brought the concept of diesel power off the branch lines, out of the switch-yards, and on to the main-lines of America's railroads. Now, see what happened:

> In 1934, year of the Pioneer Zephyr's birth, American railroads employed approximately 50,000 steam locomotives to produce 17.8 billion passenger-miles and 268 billion ton-miles of rail transportation. In 1961, when 28,500 diesel units did the work, the railroad plant turned out 20 billion passenger-miles and 565 billion ton-miles.

In summary, two factors deserve major emphasis: The diesel can pull a longer, heavier train . . . and the diesel is ready and able to work practically all day, every day. In other words, to-day's diesel fulfills the promise made by the Burlington Zephyr of 1934.

Knowing all this, it is entirely reasonable to conclude that the Burlington, its early ventures with internal combustion, and the Pioneer Zephyr were the significant precursors of modern railroad technology. Thus DIESELS WEST! is a serious historical record of an important historical era. It will be placed in the hands of schools and colleges, libraries and historical associations, publishers and public leaders, shippers and travelers, our colleagues in the transportation industry and the interested public at large.

But please remember this: The Burlington diesel story confirms the fact that progress never ends. And so it is representative of all American railroads—the only privately-owned, self-supporting, tax-paying mass transportation establishment in our nation.

H. C. MURPHY
President
Burlington Lines

Chicago, Illinois
August 27, 1963

the great God Steam

ON A DOZEN OR SO weekends each year, the Chicago, Burlington & Quincy disproves the old saw that corporations are soulless creatures by firing up a steam locomotive, coupling her to an excursion train filled with several hundred appreciative railroad buffs, and once again covering the countryside with the romance of fancy whistling and rapid exhaust.

For a few hours on these summer Sundays the present is repealed and the past is recalled as eight-coupled driving wheels accelerate to a mile a minute and black smoke smudges the tinted glass of Vista-Dome cars. Microphones hung in the slatted doors of the baggage car behind the engine commit to tape every decibel of the steamer's going, and dozens of cameras are focused upon her each time she pauses for water or a special photo stop. For the fans know that there is not a single steam locomotive left in regularly scheduled mainline railroad service anywhere in America and that only through the sympathetic cooperation of a line such as the Burlington can steam be heard and seen today. Which might seem strange indeed, because the Burlington itself introduced high-speed diesel railroading to the country in 1934—and became totally dieselized in 1958.

Fortunately for the fans, a man who worked as hard as anyone to implement and to prove the diesel has not allowed statistics to swallow up sentiment. Burlington President Harry C. Murphy, who contributed to many an early management decision for diesels, is the first to acknowledge that the blast of air horns is to the heart no substitute for the mellow chime of a steam whistle, and it is at his personal direction that the railroad keeps a pair of serviceable steam engines on the property.

They constitute significant memorabilia of an era eclipsed by the Zephyr, for one of them, Mikado type O-1A No. 4960,

was added to the roster in 1923 when the Burlington's steam ownership hit a peak of 1978 engines; and the other, Northern O-5B No. 5632, was completed in the road's West Burlington (Ia.) Shops in August, 1940, just two months before the company acquired its last new steam power. Though shelved by a technological revolution with which they could not keep pace, Nos. 4960 and 5632 were, in their own context of steam, dependable performers. Today the sight of one galloping along the banks of the Mississippi stirs the heart of a Burlington man, because steam was the common denominator of his road for almost a century—from the company's humble origins in 1850 as a 12-mile Illinois short line propelled by a hand-me-down 10-ton engine to its present status of an 11-state, 8648-mile system whose name is a household word from Lake Michigan to the Rockies.

Pioneer, the name that was destined to prefix the world's most famous streamliner, was also the moniker of the tiny funnel-stacked and pot-bellied wood-burner that puffed out of Batavia, Ill., at 6:30 a.m. on September 2, 1850, with a single wooden coach to inaugurate service over the first 6 miles of what was destined to be the initial link in today's Burlington Route. The top-hatted dignitaries who rode along in the Pioneer's fiery smoke nursed no grandiose dreams of railroad empire building. They had simply chartered the Aurora Branch Railroad from its namesake town in the Fox River Valley to Turner Junction, a distance of 12 miles, and arranged for trackage rights beyond to the young city of Chicago (1850 population: 29,963) over the connecting Galena & Chicago Union. Indeed, the G&CU owned both the Pioneer and the coach which initiated Aurora Branch service; the new line was borrowing them pending delivery of its own equipment.

7

Something of the nature of railroading on the Burlington's oldest antecedent may be judged by the fact that the single-drivered Pioneer carried just 100 pounds steam pressure. She was the creation of one-time jeweler Matthias W. Baldwin, America's first successful locomotive builder, and she had been fashioned in his shop on Broad Street, Philadelphia, in 1836. The engine had worked on both the Utica & Schenectady and the Michigan Central before being shipped westward on a sailing vessel to become, on the G&CU, Chicago's first iron horse. On loan to the Aurora Branch, the veteran jostled along on strap rail—thin strips of iron laid on 6-inch-square lengths of pine, spiked in turn to the crossties.

As crude as that notable journey on September 2, 1850, appears in retrospect, it nevertheless contained the essentials of the impending century of steam. The theory was there—a power unit and trailing vehicles, fitted with the built-in guidance system of flanged wheels, employing the adhesion of iron on iron for power and speed and braking. The gauge, 4 feet 8½ inches between the insides of the rail heads, was destined to become the national standard. And the Pioneer was very much the prototype, however rudimentary, of the latter-day 4960 and 5632; all three have in common a horizontal firetube boiler with firebox and cab on the rear end and two cylinders under the front, with the reciprocating motion transmitted to the driving wheels by side rods. All in steam that followed the Pioneer was evolutionary in principle. The revolution in motive power would have to await the successful adaptation of internal-combustion power to railroad usage.

Yet if the principle of steam locomotion remained the same until dieselization, its application did not; even a cursory review of Chicago, Burlington & Quincy* locomotives

*A merger of three lines, including the Aurora Branch, adopted th name in 1855 and by the following year, the designation was an exa description of its map.

proves the point well. Throughout the Civil War and during its immediate aftermath, the growing system standardized on the all-purpose and aptly-named American, or 4-4-0, type (*i.e.*, a four-wheel engine or guiding truck; four coupled driving wheels; and no trailing wheels). This engine could lug freight or wheel passengers, burn wood or coal (CB&Q began to switch fuels in 1857), and maintain a creditable average speed of 30 miles per hour with the wooden expresses of the day. But beginning in the 1880's the road's now-famous dissatisfaction with the status quo began to make itself felt.

In 1885 Aurora Shops completed a dynamometer car that could accurately test an engine's pulling efficiency. During 1886-1887 the company sponsored an elaborate series of braking tests on its West Burlington (Ia.) hill site; as a result

9

George Westinghouse patented his triple-valve fully automatic air brake—the tool which as much as larger power made longer, faster trains possible. In 1888 the Burlington took delivery on the first of its famous H-class Moguls. Successively refined models of these 2-6-0's were soon performing extraordinary feats. In April, 1895 one of them raced the six-car Fast Mail from Chicago to Galesburg, Ill., 162.5 miles, in 165 minutes, including three slow orders and three stops; in 1897 the Moguls helped to speed a passenger special from Chicago to Denver, 1026 miles, in 18 hours 53 minutes; and in 1900 a 2-6-0 averaged 73.6 miles per hour, start to stop, from Mendota to Aurora, Ill., 45.4 miles.

At the turn of the century steam was breaking records faster than the enthusiastic trade papers could set them in type. A pair of experimental Atlantic (4-4-2 wheel arrangement) "greyhounds," as they were quickly dubbed in song and advertising, with enormous driving wheels 84¼ inches in diameter, were delivered by Baldwin. These speedsters

11

were compounds, using their steam first in high-pressure cylinders, then in low-pressure cylinders, and the pace they could make was limited only by the signals ahead and the engineer's nerve. Moreover, they managed to pile up more than 10,000 miles a month each.

Speed won mail contracts, produced bold headlines, and attracted the public—but as Burlington steamed into the 20th century the key to its destiny lay in development of more powerful freight locomotives, engines that could accommodate the tidal wave of foodstuffs and livestock off the prairies. In 1860 a fledgling 310-mile Burlington had carried 407,314 tons of freight; by 1900 the 7545-mile road was moving more than 15,000,000 tons a year; and in 1920 a 9371-mile CB&Q could be called upon to haul more than 47,000,000 tons! Stated another way, the average revenue load behind the engine of a CB&Q freight in 1860 had been 115 tons, a figure which climbed 72 per cent to a load of 198 tons by 1900. Yet by 1920 the average load would be 676 tons—or 241 per cent more than at the turn of the century!

This awesome challenge could not be met by simply enlarging boilers, raising steam pressure, and adding more driving wheels. First the track structure, foundation of any railroad, had to be equal to the demands of the mechanical department. As early as 1899 the Burlington constructed a treating plant at Edgemont, S. Dak., to chemically protect wooden ties from weather and insect decay as well as from the splitting action of spikes. Across the following 20 years the entire CB&Q was relaid with treated ties and average tie life was increased from 7.3 years to more than 20. The primitive strap rail which the Pioneer trod on the Aurora Branch in 1850 quickly gave way to the T-shaped iron rail in 1853, and the first Bessemer steel rails were spiked down in 1867.

As engines grew heavier (from 36-ton Americans to 64½-ton H-class Moguls to 79½-ton compound Atlantics), Burlington civil and maintenance of way engineers had to anticipate each change with longer turntables and sidings, stronger bridges, heavier rail.

Burlington power continued to grow so rapidly that no intelligent man dared predict its ultimate size. For example, in 1899 CB&Q originated and aptly named the Prairie type, a 2-6-2 whose six 64-inch drivers provided an efficient balance of power and speed and whose pair of rear trailing wheels permitted a larger, wider firebox than those of older engines, which cramped narrow fireboxes between their driving wheels.

Between 1899 and 1906 successive versions of the Prairie jumped 54 per cent in weight and 60 per cent in tractive effort—and still Chicago headquarters had no recourse but to besiege the builders for bigger power. Shortened schedules and new all-steel equipment necessitated bigger passenger engines. Coal from southern Illinois mines, the heaviest and most abundant of the commodities moved by Burlington, also demanded more powerful locomotives, as did the tight curves and steep grades of the Black Hills District. Confronted with such specialized requirements for larger locomotives, the railroad relegated the all-purpose Prairie to secondary and branch-line service and began tailoring the power to the job.

In 1906 the first Pacific, or 4-6-2, appeared in passenger service; and in 1910 the Mikado, or 2-8-2, began a highly successful systemwide term of service as an all-around freight engine that would last for almost a half century. Mallets, essentially two engines under one boiler with the forward one pivoted to halve the rigid wheelbase and provide for articulation around sharp curves, joined the roster in 1908 in the shape of compound 2-6-6-2's; in 1911 there even appeared the 2-8-8-2 type. Finally in 1912 the Baldwin Locomotive Works of Philadelphia, the predominant builder of Burlington power from the Pioneer until the end of steam, furnished a veritable landmark in CB&Q locomotive design.

The engine was a 2-10-2, No. 6000, which, with a total engine weight without tender of more than 189 tons, ranked as the heaviest nonarticulated locomotive in the world. The Santa Fe-type engine (named after the road which first used the wheel arrangement) was such a giant that its center driving wheels were "blind" (i.e., without flanges) to ease it through curves, and its 88 square feet of grate area (compared with 55 square feet of the largest Prairie type built only six years before) made a mechanical stoker mandatory. So big, in fact, was this 2-10-2 that just one of its 10 driving axles carried more than three times the entire weight of the little

Pioneer!

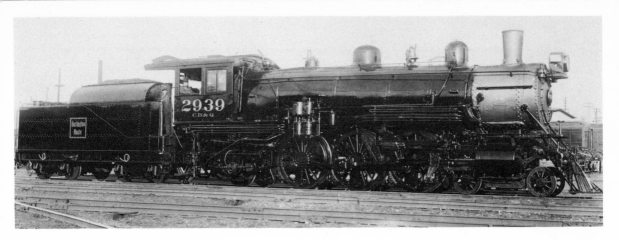

A Santa Fe's performance in drag freight service was as rewarding as its dimensions were startling, for a single 2-10-2 could be counted upon to plod along at 30 miles per hour with a 6000-ton coal train of 90 cars tied to its tender. It was with understandable pride that railroad and builder displayed a sister engine, No. 6110, in 1915 at the Panama-Pacific Exposition in San Francisco.

Such strides in size were predicated upon the refinement of existing components and the invention of auxiliary aids to efficiency, including lightweight rods and reciprocating parts, roller bearings, automatic stokers, superheaters, power reverse gears, feedwater heaters, and mechanical lubrication. Such improvements made it possible to pull more—faster and longer, as in the case of 4-8-2 Mountain type passenger engines which, by 1925, were handling limiteds of up to 22 cars at average speeds of 40 miles per hour on runs of 485 miles without change.

In terms of speed, power, and efficiency, Burlington steam power entered its finest and final stage in the years 1927 and 1930. From the Eddystone (Pa.) erecting halls of Baldwin there arrived in 1927 the 2-10-4 type (called the Texas by most roads but dubbed the heavy Santa Fe or Colorado by the Burlington). Three years later came both the Hudson, or 4-6-4, and the Northern, or 4-8-4. Each of the three merits a paragraph, not alone for the improvement it constituted over existing engines, but because these three stood for the high-water mark in steam that the diesel would have to top to make good.

The M-4 class 2-10-4 was the Burlington's first "superpower" locomotive, as the breed was known in the late 1920's. The steam locomotive had virtually reached the maximum practical clearance and axle loading limits of well constructed main lines, so it became imperative that the engine's designers achieve greater efficiency with only modest increases in weight on drivers and over-all height, width, and wheelbase. Although the 2-10-4 was a substantially heavier engine than its predecessor 2-10-2 (with an engine weight of 256 tons vs. 194.3 for the older unit), it weighed only marginally more on drivers (353,820 vs. 310,600 pounds) because of a four-wheel trailing truck which not only bore much of the weight but supported a vastly enlarged firebox. And any steam locomotive, no matter what size its boiler, is limited by its firing rate—that is, how fast it can convert coal into heat. The newcomer, then, not only could start a heavier train but could produce the sustained horsepower to keep it moving at a gait that would have quickly winded the older machine. In comparative tests the super-power M-4's took 8000-ton coal trains from Centralia to Beardstown, Ill., 135 miles, in 2 hours less time than a 2-10-2 required with 6800 tons—and did the job on 16 per cent less coal and 22 per cent less water.

Although built as coal haulers, all of the 18 2-10-4's were rebuilt prior to the war as M-4A's by the application of disc main drivers, light-weight rods and reciprocating parts (to reduce dynamic augment), and roller bearings; as a result, these engines gave excellent accounts of themselves in fast and exacting mainline service, including turns on troop trains. The 2-10-4's were compact in appearance despite their size, and possibly ranked as the system's most photogenic steam locomotives. Additionally, when originally built, they were among the world's most powerful two-cylinder locomotives.

Titleholders, too, were the dozen S-4 class Hudson-type engines built by Baldwin in 1930, for they then ranked as the world's heaviest and most powerful 4-6-4's. These splendid machines were capable of running more than 100 miles per

hour, could handle 15 or more conventional steel cars, averaged a bit more than 12,000 miles each a month (and up to
16,500 miles in 30 days in one instance), and were operated
from Chicago to McCook, Nebr., 779 miles, without change.

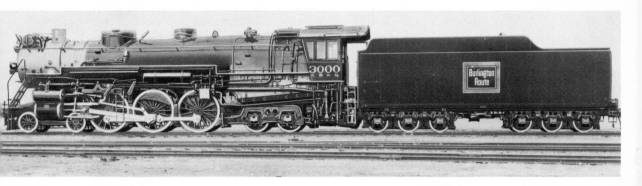

Their true capacity, however, was to await the competitive
challenge of the diesel. In 1937 the Burlington was seeking
a suitable stand-by protection engine for the expanding
Zephyr fleet. The West Burlington Shops fitted S-4 No.
3002 with lightweight roller-bearing rods and roller bearings
on driving and trailing truck axles, applied a stainless-steel
shroud of more or less Zephyr styling, and added the name
Aeolus (from the deity in Greek mythology who was the
"keeper of the winds"). In addition, the Q reclassed and re-
numbered the engine S-4A 4000. On several occasions
Aeolus (or just "Big Alice the Goon," as railroaders affec-
tionately subtitled her) had a go with the streamliners. Her
finest hour was when she sped from St. Paul to Chicago,
431 miles, on the Morning Zephyr, spent just 38 minutes
in the roundhouse for routine servicing, then roared west
1034 miles without change on the Denver Zephyr.

So impressed was the railroad that West Burlington Shops
itself built a sister streamlined Aeolus, No. 4001, in 1938 and
rebuilt three more S-4's into S-4A's, though without shrouds.

19

All of the Hudsons did yeoman service throughout the early
1940's on war-swollen limiteds, and (just ask any Burlington
man) what one of these 4-6-4's couldn't do with a redball
livestock train was just nobody's business. So long as anyone
on the railroad recalls steam, from President Murphy on
down, the S-4's will get into the conversation.

The Burlington's very best in steam, though, was the O-5 class Northern, or 4-8-4, type. Baldwin built the first eight O-5's in 1930 and West Burlington Shops constructed 28 more during the years 1937, 1938 and 1940. The forte of

21

the O-5 was this: she was neither strictly a freighter like the M-4 nor a passenger engine like the S-4, but a dual-purpose machine that could do either job. On most divisions of the railroad the O-5 was rated at 3000 to 3500 tons in scheduled freight service. In passenger service the same engine worked easily up to 80 miles per hour, and during the depression O-5's regularly worked between Chicago and St. Paul with the combined Empire Builder-North Coast Limited totaling 23 steel cars.

In short, the O-5 was that rare breed of locomotive that dispatchers, shop workers, officials, enginemen, and accountants could all agree upon. She steamed and rode well, kept repair and fuel costs down, seldom faltered, was as much at home in the Galesburg freight yard as in Chicago Union Station, and sounded off with a sharp exhaust that no one recalls today with more pleasure than does the Burlington's president. During the last two decades of steam power development in America, more roads invested in Northern-type locomotives than in any other single wheel arrangement, and there were exceptional 4-8-4's on roads ranging from New York Central to Southern Pacific. Few Burlington men would debate the merits of the others, so strong is their faith that in the O-5 they possessed the finest of them all.

In October, 1940, West Burlington Shops assembled the railroad's last new steam locomotive, O-5A No. 5635. There was no publicity attendant to the day on which the first fire was laid upon the grates of the Burlington's last 4-8-4. At the time, the Burlington owned more than 1000 steam engines, and even the most enthusiastic supporters of the company's Zephyrs and tiny fleet of diesel switchers were unwilling to publicly predict an end to the era the Pioneer had begun in 1850. Yet within five years the advancing technology of internal combustion power was destined to make a dinosaur of the 5635.

Retirement:
Locomotive No. 3003
on permanent display
at Burlington, Ia.

first Rumblings

IT BEGAN as a speck on the prairie horizon, a dot where the light branch-line rails joined at infinity. It grew nearer at a modest 30 miles per hour—and became a squarish flat front end, painted red and yellow and breathing just a trace of blue exhaust. And then its grumbling engine subsided into an idle, and with offset bell tolling, the Pullman green car with the vividly painted nose eased up to the brick platform and bay window of the red frame country depot.

It was the daily-except-Sunday local, a self-propelled train-in-one-car. Within an over-all length of just 75 feet, it provided space for a Railway Post Office, baggage and express, 24 passengers, and its own locomotion. For a generation such gas-electric motor cars—promptly nicknamed "doodle-bugs" by the candid—were as familiar to the heartland of America as tall corn, and the honk of their air horns at station mile boards was the event of the day in many a rural hamlet. Small boys would gather at cabside to talk to the white-capped engineer and to peer in at the 6-cylinder, 275-horsepower gasoline engine-generator power plant that kept him company. Meantime, mail sacks were exchanged, the express messenger dropped off a new bicycle and accepted cartons of squeaky baby chicks, and the conductor exchanged confidences with the agent. Then (and it was always all too soon) the conductor studied his watch, raised an arm toward the engineer, and stepped up into the vestibule at the rear of the car. The gas engine barked and the doodlebug trundled off down the branch and across the horizon.

The Burlington owned more of these gas-electric passenger motor cars—57 of them—than any other railroad in the country. Costing less to operate than steam trains, Burlington doodlebugs saved enough to pay for themselves. What's more, long before the automobile emptied their green plush seats, they girded the Q with experience which would be invaluable when the Zephyrs entered the picture. They ran off more than 3.6 million miles a year and cost just 35 cents a mile to operate (compared with 56 cents a mile for the steam schedules they replaced). Spanning the system from Aurora to Denver, they registered an astonishing availability record of 94 per cent—high enough to dispatch 192 old 4-4-0 and 4-6-0 steamers to the cutting torch. Burlington motor cars ranged in weight from 58 to 69 tons and frequently pulled trailers; they were powered by 6- or 8-cylinder gas engines of 225 to 400 horsepower, connected to generators that produced direct current for truck-mounted electric traction motors. Light preventive maintenance was usually sufficient to keep heavy overhauls up to 230,000 miles and two years apart. Though modest of gait and humble in appearance, the doodlebugs contained all of the essential ingredients of the coming motive power revolution that would retire steam forever.

The Burlington actually put together a crude grand-daddy of the gas-electric car as early as 1898. The prime mover (as well as the undoing) of the railcar that Aurora Shops built was a bulky 3-cylinder gas engine which was supposed to develop 100 horsepower at 240 r.p.m. Trouble was, the huge flywheel accounted for 5000 pounds of the engine's 12,000 pound total weight and it produced so much vibration that various parts as well as the car's chain-drive transmission literally flew apart. The crankshaft was re-counter-balanced to compensate but, to quote one report, "even then the terrific detonation, due to inadequate cooling and poor combustion, caused cylinder heads, valves and pistons to break; in fact, these parts would get so hot that the best metal available at that time would warp, crystallize, and fail in a short time."

The Burlington bided its time for a quarter-century—until 1922, when it invested $17,500 in a Mack truck chassis with flanged wheels and bus-type passenger body. The following year, it added a couple of tiny (8½ ton, 45-horsepower) direct-drive gas railcars, which replaced steam trains out of Atchison, Kans., to Rulo, Nebr., and Armour, Mo. When these cars cut operating costs in half, the Burlington promptly bought six more gas-mechanical cars of a larger design. These 43-footers weighed 21½ tons and mounted a 6-cylinder, 90-horsepower engine in each truck, which left the carbody clear to accommodate 40 passengers and their baggage. The cars ran well enough to earn themselves a secure niche in the Burlington's timetable, but their mechanical transmissions did leave something to be desired. First, they were not quite robust enough for the weight they had to move. And second, they had the embarrassing habit of occasionally failing to co-ordinate the car's two engines so that when the throttle was opened up, the trucks would tug

in opposite directions, much to the amusement of the depot bystanders and the discomfiture of the crew.

So far as the Burlington was concerned, the motor car came of age in 1927 when the railroad began buying gas-electric equipment from the Electro-Motive Company. EMC was actually just a small office in Cleveland, O., populated with a few bright minds. Its only product was an idea. EMC designed, sold, and serviced dependable standardized gas-electrics. Having no factory of its own, EMC subcontracted the gasoline 6- and 8-cylinder engines of its cars to Winton, their electrical transmissions to General Electric or Westinghouse, and their bodies to such carbuilders as Pullman and St. Louis Car. All components were built to EMC's specifications, though, and the tiny firm's own mechanics

and parts depots stood behind each car that carried its builder plate. Thus began a rewarding association between Burlington and Electro-Motive that was destined not only to endure to this day but also to revolutionize railroad motive power everywhere.

The kind of EMC performance that impressed the railroad was typified by cars 9627 and 9628, which operated as local trains No. 1 and 2 between Keokuk and Shenandoah, Ia.—a 244-mile run each way which included 47 stops and consumed 10 hours 18 minutes. Every other night each car got home to Keokuk where a single mechanic took care of all its servicing needs in 4 hours. Between them, the two gas-electrics, each hauling a passenger trailer, saved the Burlington more than $100 over comparable steam-train costs each day they operated. They breezed past water tanks and coaling towers, required no ash pits, rumbled through drifting snow with aplomb, and never put a cinder in anybody's eye.

In 1930, the Burlington added another notch to its not inconsiderable gas-electric experience with an odd little creature which, in appearance, couldn't seem to make up its mind which way to go. No. 7168 was technically a locomotive, but no CB&Q roundhouse had ever housed its like. It possessed a steeple cab mounted amidships on a stubby 29-foot frame. Sloping downward on each end was a truck-like radiator-fronted hood. Each hood enclosed a 6-cylinder, 165-horsepower gasoline engine coupled to a generator which fed power to a pair of axle-hung electric traction motors in each truck. The 330-horsepower, 45-ton midget was unpretentiousness itself, but then, the Burlington hadn't bought it for looks.

In Crete, Nebr., the railroad served a number of industries on a daily yard trick that wasn't busy enough to justify a full-time steam yard engine yet entailed too much work for as-

29

signment to passing local freight trains. One day Crete's regular switcher, an elderly 0-6-0, was allowed to cool down, and the steeple-cab oddity burbled about doing the work instead. And whereas Burlington had spent $55.37 to operate the steamer, the road found that No. 7168 cost just $21.06. For example, the steam engine usually burned a bit better than 5½ tons of coal a day; cost: $23.86. However, just $4.42 purchased enough gasoline to accomplish the same work with the 7168. One morning the 7168 even got venturesome enough to replace a K-2 class 4-6-0 steam locomotive on a 9-hour local freight round trip between Keokuk and Mt. Pleasant, Ia. Cost per trip for the gas-electric, $27.95; for the 4-6-0, $54.77.

A larger 60-ton, 450-horsepower gas-electric locomotive of similar steeple-cab appearance joined the roster in March 1932 and was stationed in Nebraska City, Nebr., where it took over work previously requiring at least the part-time use of three steam engines. Daily except Sunday, the engine handled the switching chores there for 8 hours, then spent the balance of the day handling a mixed freight-and-passenger train on the 6-mile branch from Nebraska City to Payne, Ia. Pleased with the unit's behavior, the Burlington bought three 65-ton, 460-horsepower steeple-cab diesel-electrics in 1933 (the first was exhibited at the Century of Progress Exposition that year in Chicago) and asked them to do something which no steam locomotive on its roster was capable of doing. The trio was assigned to yard service 24 hours a day 6 days a week, and 16 hours on the 7th day. They were fueled during crew changes; all maintenance had to be accomplished during just 8 hours per week. The new diesel-electrics not only met this rigorous assignment, but cost the company $2 per yard engine-hour compared with $4.22 for the steam engines they replaced.

Thus step by step, from gas-mechanical railcars to gas-electric motor cars to gas- and finally diesel-electric switchers, the Burlington felt its way cautiously and yet surely into the unexplored world of nonsteam railroading. True, all of these self-propelled passenger "doodlebugs" and midget steeple-cab engines couldn't hold a candle in appearance to the World's Fair train which Burlington proudly exhibited in 1933 at Chicago's Century of Progress Exposition. Heading this six-car sampling of equipment from such CB&Q limiteds as the Aristocrat and Black Hawk was what the railroad itself termed "a great Leviathan of the rail," Hudson-type steam engine No. 3000. The huge 4-6-4 weighed 359 tons with its tender and certainly looked fierce enough to

31

have eaten alive any puttering doodlebug that might have dared venture into its path. Yet as subsequent events were to prove, the Leviathan was even then the last member of a great race of steam passenger engines. Within a year the seeds of technology within the humble gas-electrics were to give birth to a radically new type of train, a train destined to make of the 3000 a museum piece.

In 1933 the Biblical prediction "But many that are first shall be last; and the last shall be first" (Matthew 19:30) was about to be fulfilled on the Burlington.

three Men, one Idea

3 DIESELS WEST!

NEVER LET IT BE SAID that the engineering mind plays favorites. Consider the automobile and the train. Some of the very men who transformed a backfiring joke of a horseless carriage into safe, dependable everyman's transportation (and thereby persuaded America to desert the railroad for the paved highway) turned right around and applied their creative technology to the train (thereby saving its life). It's a fascinating story which stars an inventor, a manufacturer, and a railroad man, and the fact that this true tale reaches an exhilarating climax in the depths of the country's worst depression renders it no less dramatic.

It is very much a Burlington story.

It began in the Twenties, for it was then that the country fell in love with the Model T and that redoubtable vehicle chugged off with the railroads' riders. The Burlington's experience was typical; year by year its annual reports recorded the impact of the gas engine and the pneumatic tire. The Burlington was carrying 18 million passengers a year on its plush seats in 1924 but only 13.8 million by 1929 and finally a mere 7 million in the worst year of the financial panic, 1933. Passenger revenues tobogganed from 28.5 million dollars in 1923 to 6.7 million in 1933.

One man saw in these figures challenge instead of chaos. Soft-spoken, bespectacled Ralph Budd took over the president's office at Burlington's headquarters in 1932. Budd, a protege of "the Empire Builder," James J. Hill, had attained the presidency of the Great Northern in 1919. There he had climaxed his administration with the construction of the 7.79-mile Cascade Tunnel, the longest tunnel in the Western Hemisphere. It was characteristic of the man that he was able to forge an even greater career out of the depression years than he had during the growth decade preceding, and his attitude toward plummeting

| Ralph Budd | Edward G. Budd, Sr. | Charles F. Kettering |

Burlington passenger receipts was typical of why he was destined to become the industry's ranking statesman.

Budd reasoned that since automobile engineers had derailed the passenger train, they should be asked to put it back on the tracks. Such thinking, of course, implied internal combustion power instead of the steam locomotive, upon which the industry had relied for a century; but Budd knew something about that, too. He had observed the trials, tribulations, and eventual triumph of the gas-electric railcars with interest. During his term as president, the Great Northern had purchased a diesel-electric switching locomotive as early as 1926 and had installed auxiliary diesel-electric stationary power plants during the building of the Cascade Tunnel. In 1930 the biggest automaker of them all, General Motors, took over both the Winton Engine Company and Winton's largest customer, railcarbuilder Electro-Motive. And in 1932 the Edward G. Budd Manufacturing Company of Philadelphia, famous for having pioneered the all-steel automobile wheel as well as the first all-steel automobile body, began considering the idea of a radically different carbody structure for passenger trains.

Ralph Budd saw and heard—and acted. He went to Philadelphia and there observed a small gas-powered, rubber-tired railcar built by the Budd Company. The car's design was unimportant—its direct-drive propulsion and pneumatic wheels were patently impractical—but its construction was arresting. The car was built entirely of stainless steel, which had chromium as its essential alloying agent. Now, stainless steel was extremely lightweight, yet incredibly strong—non-abrasive and corrosion-free. In the past, though, nobody had ever been able to reduce the high-tensile alloy to a practical shop operation because it could not be easily or dependably fabricated. But the rivetless seams of the railcar had been joined by Budd's newly patented Shotweld process—a system which not only preserved the corrosion-resistant qualities of the metal but actually produced a joint stronger than the adjoining steel. Ralph Budd instantly recognized the worth of Shotwelded stainless steel to railroading: it was a metal that would last throughout the entire service life of the rolling stock which was built of it. Stainless steel cost more, yes—but as Budd knew, the maintenance cost of a railroad car exceeds its purchase price in its useful lifetime. Reduced repairs, then, should more than offset the higher initial cost.

But what type of train? Budd was thinking, in his own words, of "situations where some train had to be operated but earnings were insufficient for any profit." About 25 per cent of Burlington passenger-train mileage at that time was operated by two-to-five-car locals, gas-electric or steam powered. A natural route lay between Kansas City and Lincoln, 250 miles. A lightweight speedster would be able to leave Lincoln about 8 a.m., be in Kansas City by noon, and return in the afternoon. Grades and curves in the territory were light; there were only six intermediate railroad grade crossings to inhibit speed. The new train would have to seat 70 or so passengers, hold 25 tons of express and baggage, and provide a mail compartment; it would be self-propelled.

On June 17, 1933 (the year President Roosevelt closed the banks and the N.R.A. was born and Germany left the League of Nations and the 18th Amendment to the Constitution was repealed) Burlington signed a contract with the Budd Company for a new-type train for the Kansas City-Lincoln run. Such was the faith that Ralph Budd had in Edward G. Budd, Sr. (the white-haired, white-mustached Philadelphia manufacturer was no kin to the railroader except in initiative) that he gave the carbuilder carte blanche in the design of the train. The only reservations were that the equipment should meet the standard gauge of 4 feet $8\frac{1}{2}$ inches, conform to standard railroad clearances, and be as safe as, if not safer than, existing passenger equipment.

The construction of the new train was soon to be profoundly influenced by another result of Ralph Budd's inherent curiosity. He heard about a problem, and about the man picked to solve it. The problem was born of the fact that the railroads were demanding more horsepower from railcarbuilder Electro-Motive than gas engines could economically produce in view of the rising price of gasoline. Winton Engine attempted spark-ignited, distillate-burning power plants, but it proved all but impossible to mix the heavy fuel with air in a carburetor and then force it under high pressure through long feed pipes to the cylinders. Yet the alternative diesel engine of the day, in which fuel oil and air were mixed

38

inside the cylinder and ignition was caused by the heat of compression alone, was a slow-speed obese creature that weighed 60 pounds or more for each horsepower it produced. General Motors research was brought to bear upon the problem when the automaker absorbed EMC and Winton in 1930; that, in turn, put Charles W. ("Boss Ket") Kettering, GM's Vice President of Research, into the picture.

Kettering thought this: "Make a diesel the way it wants to be made." In terms of Ket's now legendary rule-of-thumb engineering, that meant throwing away precedent and convention and trying new injection methods, air supply systems, pistons, crankshafts, and blocks—and then letting the engine, by its performance, dictate which components worked best.

Out of GM's research came the two-cycle diesel. Gasoline and early diesel engines were four-stroke power plants. That is, the first downward stroke of the piston sucked in air, which was compressed by the second, or return, stroke of the piston. At this point the injector shot in a spray of fuel, which—mixing with the compressed air—ignited, forcing the piston down on its third, or power, stroke. The fourth and final stroke of the piston forced the burned gases out the exhaust-valve ports. Now, the two-stroke engine worked the same way so far as compression, injection of fuel, and expansion were concerned; the key difference was that fresh air entered the cylinder as the exhaust gases were leaving it, thus providing one power stroke for each two strokes of the piston, instead of one-for-four. Fundamental changes were necessary to success of the two-stroke principle. For example, lacking a complete air-intake stroke, the two-cycle engine required an external blower to force air into its cylinders since it could not act as its own air pump.

Eventually the tiny one-cylinder prototypes of two-cycle

39

diesel design proved successful enough in GM's labs to warrant construction of an 8-cylinder, 600-horsepower engine (which produced a startling weight-to-power ratio of just 20 pounds per horsepower). Actually, two such engines were built and sent to Chicago, where they furnished the power for the GM Building at the Century of Progress Exposition.

And that is where Ralph Budd encountered them. He knew, to be sure, that a stationary diesel running at constant speed in clean surroundings has nothing in common, environmentally, with one experiencing the vibration and dirt of stop-and-go railroad service. He knew, too, that GM had, in effect, all of Lake Michigan to cool its two-cycle engines at the World's Fair site. And he was aware of the nightmarish problems the newcomers kept creating for their mechanics. (Kettering put it this way: "Let it suffice to say that I do not remember any trouble with the dip stick.")

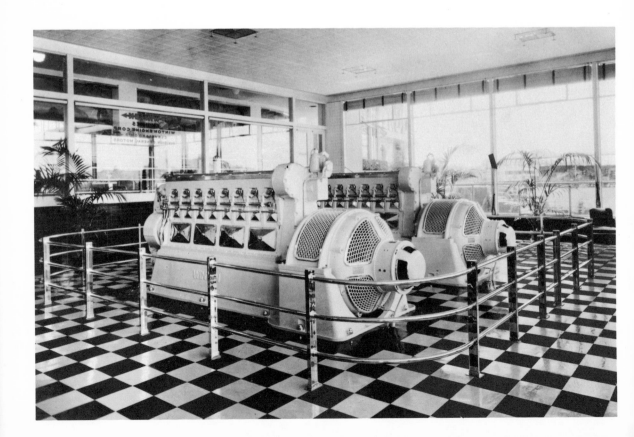

Yet diesel power was inevitable, and sooner or later GM could make it practical if anyone could. So Ralph Budd, whom Ket described as a "very nervy railroad president," asked for a diesel engine for his new train. Budd saw it this way: "I knew that if General Motors was willing to put the engine in a train, the national spotlight would be on the Corporation. They'd simply have to stay with it until it was satisfactory. I knew they'd make good. Actually, I wasn't taking a chance at all."

On April 7, 1934, the Burlington's new train—America's first diesel-powered streamlined train—emerged from its cocoon in Philadelphia, and two days later hit 104 miles per hour on a brief trial trip out to Perkiomen Junction, Pa., 24.8 miles. The silvery streamliner, numbered 9900, was like nothing else on rails anywhere.

No. 9900 stretched 196 feet from its slanted nose to its rounded solarium-lounge and weighed in at just 97½ tons.

41

It had three carbody units but because of the articulated design (*i.e.*, the ends of the center car rode on the same trucks as the inner ends of the power and observation bodies) the effect was snakelike. The roof line and carbody sides were smooth, unbroken by the vestibules of ordinary coaches; passengers entered by center doorways on each car. In the lead car was the operator's cab, a 600-horsepower diesel-generator set (which delivered direct-current to two traction motors on the lead truck), a Railway Post Office, and a mail storage compartment. The second car contained space for 50,000 pounds of baggage and express, a buffet-grill, and 20 seats. The third car had 40 more seats, as well as a 12-passenger observation-lounge in the tail.

The appointments and styling of No. 9900 were the responsibility of the architectural firms of Paul Cret and Holabird & Root. They poured into the three-car train all the modernity no one associated with railroad trains in 1934: indirect lighting, pastel shades of warm gray and green, silk window drapes, airconditioning, meal-at-your-seat trays, carpeted aisles, even radio reception.

The 9900's engineering was just as revolutionary. In orthodox railroad cars the frame of the car is its backbone, but the 9900's tubular construction enabled the entire carbody to possess load-bearing functions. Sides and particularly the roof thus comprised major structural members. And, of course, the entire train was produced of stainless steel—Shotwelded and almost three times as strong as ordinary steel.

The heart of No. 9900 was its two-cycle, 8-cylinder, inline Winton diesel—a redesign of the World's Fair power plant Budd had observed the year before and very much the handiwork of "Boss Ket." It was technically billed as the 201A engine, and upon its performance No. 9900 stood to win or lose. As a matter of fact, the train's delivery had been delayed several weeks so that the diesel engine could be installed instead of a spark-ignition distillate Winton. Honors for the first streamliner in the land had gone to Union Pacific back on February 12 when that road had taken delivery of a three-car articulated aluminum train, the M10000 (later the City of Salina), which was powered by a Winton 600-horsepower, V-12 distillate engine. CB&Q's 9900, then, was the first diesel-electric streamliner as well as the first stainless-steel train.

In the spring of 1934 no one could say with certainty whether or not a "very nervy railroad president" had urged the diesel out of its cradle too soon or even if Shotwelded stainless steel was worth its extra cost. Ahead of No. 9900 lay an extraordinary, revolutionary 15 years of railroading—1 million passengers' and 3.2 million miles' worth of it—that would forever alter trains and the locomotives that pulled them. But no one, not even Ralph Budd, knew that then.

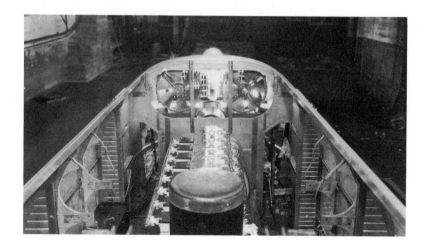

History-makers:
The City of Salina (LEFT)
and the Pioneer Zephyr,
(RIGHT) which was
first diesel-powered
streamlined train,
meet in the Kansas City
Union Station

45

No. 9900

ZEPHYR— that was the name with which No. 9900 was christened Wednesday, April 18, 1934, in the Pennsylvania Railroad's Broad Street Station, Philadelphia. It referred to the Greek personification of the West Wind; the particular reference the railroad had in mind was from the prologue to Chaucer's Canterbury Tales: "Whan Zephirus eek with his swete breeth. . . ." Much to the astonishment of *Chicago Tribune* columnist June Provines, Ralph Budd not only could explain the derivation of the word but could quote "unhesitatingly" from Chaucer—which was more surprising coming from a "hard-headed and successful railroad man," the newspaperwoman confessed, than the name Zephyr itself. Budd was also a historian. At the dedication ceremonies (at which Graham McNamee was emcee and Miss Marguerite Cotsworth, daughter of the railroad's passenger traffic manager, swung the bottle) he said, "To those of us on the railroads this sleek, glistening, streamlined streak symbolizes progress, and it is appropriate that the Burlington should build this train for use along the Missouri River, for Burlington track was the first to reach the Missouri in the railroad race for the West. This was in 1859."

The Zephyr began a five-week barnstorming tour which led to Chicago via New York, Boston, Buffalo, Cleveland, Pittsburgh, Cincinnati, Louisville. En route, the streamliner zipped across Pennsy's 140-mile speedway from Fort Wayne, Ind., to Englewood Station, Chicago, at an average speed of 80.2 miles per hour in spite of a 40 mile per hour head wind.

The big day—perhaps the most dramatic day in all Burlington history—was May 26, 1934. To signal the reopening of the Century of Progress in Chicago the railroad had agreed to attempt a nonstop record-breaking run of approximately 15 hours from Denver to Chicago. In 1934 the crack steam-powered Aristocrat took 26¾ hours for the run, albeit with 40 intermediate stops. The record stood at 18 hours 53 minutes and had been set in 1897 when the road rushed Henry J. Mayham to the bedside of his dying son in Denver. But 15 hours—that meant an average speed of 70 miles per hour! One of the Zephyr's retinue recalled that it had taken four days just to crank up the diesel when the train was hauled out of the shop in Philadelphia. Could the same eight cylinders now endure the longest, most grueling railroad run of all time? Could any engine?

Ralph Budd, whom no one ever called a gambler, calculated the answer was "Yes." And once committed, he never

hesitated. On the afternoon before the run, scheduled for departure at 4 a.m. next day, an inspector discovered a cracked armature bearing in one of No. 9900's traction motors. Much phoning turned up a similar motor in Union Pacific's shop at Omaha and that road gladly offered to pull a bearing from it for CB&Q's use. A Burlington man picked up the bearing and caught an airliner for Cheyenne, with instructions to change to a chartered plane and be in Denver at 12:30 a.m. But even as he was winging westward (and just before Ralph Budd was to leave the Denver shop for downtown to tell a nationwide radio audience about the following day's sprint) a phone call came which eased the mounting tension. Here, if you will, was the Zephyr incapacitated hours before it was supposed to break records, its slanted nose up on jacks, and over the phone the editor of the *Rocky Mountain News* was asking Burlington Vice-President Edward E. Flynn if he should bring over a Rocky Mountain canary to the shop.

"What's a Rocky Mountain canary?"

"A burro."

"A *what?*"

"A donkey—a small one."

It was actually Zeph, a gift of the paper to the Century of Progress, and he was supposed to ride east in the Zephyr's baggage compartment—a fellow-passenger of the representatives of Budd, General Motors, and other suppliers; the president of the Denver & Salt Lake; 36 Burlington officers, and 20 reporters.

Flynn asked Budd about Zeph and received the now classic reply,

"Why not? One more jackass on this trip won't make any difference."

Later on that night, with the bearing still somewhere en route, Ralph Budd spoke into a microphone: "Tomorrow at dawn we'll be on our way!"

And so they were. The bearing was in Denver shortly after midnight and in place beneath No. 9900's snout in the re-assembled power truck a few hours later. The scheduled departure hour of four o'clock came and went with no Zephyr, true, but at 5:05 a.m. Ralph Budd's "streamlined streak" was off and running. A green flag that had started 15 Memorial Day Indianapolis Speedway Races gave the starting signal on Track 1 in Denver Union Station. No. 9900's diesel revved up, and the nose of the streamliner sliced a tape to set off a Western Union electric timing clock on the platform.

Ahead lay a specially shortened route of 1015.4 miles, with a flagman stationed at each of 619 private roads and two men at each of 1070 public grade crossings. Each foot of track, every switch and signal and bridge, had been examined prior to the run. And as the train traversed four divisions en route, each superintendent would remain at the elbow of his dispatcher. In effect, more than a thousand miles of high-speed mainline railroad had been given to the Zephyr; now it was up to the god of the West Wind.

Speed was deliberately held down on the first lap to see if the new bearing would run warm, yet even so, the 78 miles to Ft. Morgan, Colo., took only 68½ minutes. Then the fun began. Screaming toward McCook, Nebr., the Zephyr averaged 90 miles per hour for 129½ straight miles, covered a 19.1-mile stretch at 106.2 miles per hour, and a 6.4-mile lap at 109 miles per hour. At one point the speedometer needle touched 112.5 miles per hour.

The strain was intense, for the success of the run depended upon every mechanical component, even every wire and pin and screw. Indeed, a broken wire almost spoiled the

run. A door slammed on an instrument wire and the resultant short circuit burned out the engine starter cable. The
engineer, smelling burning rubber and fearing a fire, shut
down the diesel engine. Frantically the technicians searched
for a wire to splice the cable and thereby restart the power,
but momentum gradually subsided until the Zephyr was
drifting at a mere 15 miles per hour. Then Electro-Motive
mechanic Roy Baer saved the day. He grabbed the ends of
the wires and held them together; there was an electrical
flash, and the engine started up. His quick, selfless act burned
his hands, but the nonstop record remained intact.

EMC's Ernie Kuehn proved himself just as alert on
another occasion when prolonged blowing of the air horn for
crossings reduced the pressure in the air brake pipe and began to apply the brakes automatically. Sensing the trouble,
Kuehn rushed to the cab and pulled the throttle wide open,
thus speeding up the air compressor and restoring air pressure. The brakes released and the Zephyr bounded ahead.

At 12:12 p.m. (C.S.T.) the streamliner passed through
Lincoln, Nebr., 482.6 miles out; by 4:38 p.m. the 9900 had
reached Burlington, Ia., and the Mississippi River; and as
the sun sank in the west the Zephyr was a flash of stainless
steel across the flat farmlands of Illinois.

At 7:10 p.m. the Zephyr broke the timing clock's tape at
Halsted Street, Chicago, having covered 1015.4 miles in 785
minutes nonstop at an average speed of 77.61 miles per hour.
Viewed by an estimated 500,000 people en route, the 13-
hour 4-minute 58-second sprint had set a world's record for
nonstop railroad running. It had also excelled all previous
records for average speeds over distances of 200 miles or
more. Actually, the Zephyr had run 215.7 miles at an average
speed of more than 90 miles per hour.

And during the entire run the two-cycle diesel had con-

51

sumed only 418 gallons of fuel—$16 worth.

The streamliner kept on rolling, via Illinois Central tracks, to the lakefront Central Station, reversed and backed to the IC's 31st Street yard, then—at 8:09 p.m.—rolled onto the stage of the Wings of a Century Pageant. And there, gleaming in the spotlights, the Zephyr stood before an exultant crowd that poured down from the amphitheater to pay it homage. For once, the crowd, which thought that such an amazing train would revolutionize the industry, fathomed more than certain practical railroaders, who were inclined to dismiss the dawn-to-dusk race as insignificant if spectacular. The Zephyr itself was destined to run more than 3 million miles, but even more important, its two-cycle diesel would breed a motive power revolution that would retire the steam locomotive permanently. That was the true significance of May 26, 1934.

No. 9900 paused just a day at the Fair, then was off on a month of exhibitions. On June 16, while en route to the Pacific Coast, the Zephyr led three Denver & Rio Grande

Western freight trains across the 38-mile Dotsero Cutoff in Colorado. This new route made it possible to incorporate the 6.2-mile Moffat Tunnel into a Denver-Utah line 175 miles shorter than the original Rio Grande main line via the Royal Gorge. Finally No. 9900 returned to the Fair.

The Zephyr, in company with UP's M10000 streamliner, spent the summer at the World's Fair, where 709,000 visitors queued up for a walk through its aisles.

In September, 1934, No. 9900, temporarily renamed the Silver Streak, traveled to Hollywood to star in an RKO film of that title. Wallace W. Abbey wrote in *Trains* Magazine

55

that "all characters, including the train, lived happily ever after." The picture's plot unfolded like this: Handsome young designer, in love with railroad president's daughter, tries to sell president on newfangled streamlined train (i.e., the Silver Streak, alias the Zephyr) but is rebuffed. . . . Train is built but at first experiences difficulty making 30 miles per hour and is ignominiously overtaken by steam engine on freight train. . . . Streamliner is on display at Fair when president's son, at work on new Boulder Dam, contracts polio, requires an iron lung (the acme of medical science in 1934). . . . Silver Streak races lung across continent even as designer and foreign spy (who wants secret of two-cycle diesel) battle each other for controls in the cab (RKO's script conveniently overlooked deadman's pedal, which would have prevented the Zephyr from running wild with nobody at the throttle). . . . Hero overcomes adversary, delivers iron lung (which saves president's son), sells streamliner to railroad, wins daughter's hand in marriage.

After Hollywood, the Zephyr made a final display tour through Texas, and then—after showing itself to more than 2 million people in 222 cities—went to work on a round trip daily between Lincoln, Omaha, St. Joseph, and Kansas City. The date was Armistice Day, 1934, and because both the UP M10000 and its new sister, the City of Portland, were still on tour, the Zephyr captured the honor of being the first streamliner in revenue service.

President Ralph Budd said of the Zephyr that "the new train would be successful if it did no more than reduce the cost of operation. If it should also stimulate travel, it would be doubly successful." In service the Zephyr replaced two steam engines and six conventional passenger cars (which weighed eight times as much as the streamliner) and operated for 34.2 cents a train-mile vs. 63.7 cents for the replaced steam trains. It also shortened schedules and boosted traffic by 150-200 per cent (vs. a systemwide passenger increase of 26 per cent for the same period). The new-type train's stainless-steel exterior never required paint, of course. No. 9900 bored right through snow, winning a better on-time reputation for itself in stormy weather than conventional trains. It was easy on the rail and could take curves comfortably 20 per cent faster than regular equipment. And the Zephyr was so popular that passengers would rather stand than take an ordinary train—indeed, so appealing that the railroad soon ordered an extra car to boost seating capacity from 72 to 112.

The great experiment of 1934 was completed; the verdict was in.

The Zephyr idea—a streamlined articulated stainless-steel train propelled by a lightweight two-cycle diesel power plant —was now ready for what Budd termed "longer and more important schedules."

THE SAGA OF THE PIONEER ZEPHYR

Gleaming stainless steel strength members and outside surfaces
assure solid long life and lasting beauty • • •

. . . Christened at Philadelphia on April 18, 1934,
the Pioneer Zephyr #9900 starts on its road to fame . . .

60

· · · May 26, 1934. The Pioneer Zephyr leaves Denver for Chicago
on its history-making, record-breaking dawn to dusk run—
averaging 77.6 miles per hour over more than 1,000 miles
—with a top speed of 112.5 · · ·

. . . A star of the 1934 Chicago Century of Progress, the Pioneer Zephyr
shares the limelight with Engine No. 35, a Burlington ancestor . . .

. . . Over 2 million people in 222 cities visited the Pioneer Zephyr
on its 30,437-mile exhibition tour . . .

. . . Movie star, too! Here's the Pioneer Zephyr during shooting for
"The Silver Streak," a hit feature film produced by RKO . . .

. . . November 11, 1934. The Pioneer Zephyr enters regular service,
making a daily round trip Lincoln-Omaha-Kansas City,
and starting a new mode of travel for all America . . .

. . . The first million Pioneer Zephyr miles are
celebrated on December 29, 1939. Now the Burlington
Zephyr fleet logs over 6,000,000 miles per year . . .

. . . Winter and summer, the Pioneer Zephyr performs
with round-the-clock efficiency. Here it slashes
through a snowdrift at high speed . . .

. . . Guest of honor at its tenth birthday party,
the Pioneer Zephyr cuts its own cake
at Lincoln, Nebr. on April 10, 1944 . . .

. . . The Pioneer Zephyr, granddaddy of diesel-powered
streamlined trains, at Quincy, Ill. celebrates
its 20th anniversary of regular service . . .

. . . May 26, 1960. On permanent display
at the Museum of Science and Industry,
Chicago, Ill. . . .

70

. . . Burlington President H. C. Murphy presents
the Pioneer Zephyr's throttle to Major Lenox R. Lohr,
President of the Museum of Science and Industry

Zephyrs unlimited

"I CAN REMEMBER," wrote Wallace W. Abbey in *Trains* Magazine, "and I do so with pleasure, driving across Iowa . . . and stopping at some out-of-the-way hamlet to watch the Zephyrs, speeding like the west wind and braying like Zeph, the burro that rode on the record trip from Denver to Chicago. It descended on us and disappeared in a swirl of dust. A frequent remark along the line was, 'She sure is coming, wasn't she?' "

All of a sudden, train riding became The New Experience for the country. Until the Zephyr, passenger trains had been as safe and sure as the steel of which they were constructed, but there was only so much that even the most prolific advertising man could say on behalf of red-plush seats and green Pullman curtains, not to mention steam locomotives. A public intrigued by automobiles and planes just wasn't listening. But the Zephyr was different, radically different. One sat in a soft individual reclining seat amidst modern, soundproofed, air-conditioned surroundings, and was effortlessly swept up to astounding speeds of 70, 80, 90—even 100 miles per hour! Riding the Zephyr was more than merely transportation in the 1930's; it was sophistication, The Thing To Do.

The Burlington couldn't order them nor could Budd build them fast enough following the enormous impact of the original Zephyr. The railroad ordered virtual duplicates of No. 9900 (except that the mail compartment was eliminated, which served to increase seating capacity from 72 to 88) for the hotly competitive Chicago-Twin Cities route.

These trains, numbered 9901 and 9902, were to be christened the Twin Zephyrs, appropriately enough, and the story of their introduction, dedication, and revenue success explains much about the fever pitch of the streamliner era. No. 9901 was completed first by the Budd Company, in the spring of 1935, so while its twin was being finished 9901 made a

whirlwind barnstorming tour of Florida over the Seaboard
Air Line. Then 9901 broke records on owner Burlington by
dashing from Chicago to St. Paul on a test run at an average
speed of 77.7 miles per hour (hitting a maximum of 104!),
and finally went as far south as Kansas City on Chamber of
Commerce specials.

On April 14 the 9901 arrived in Aurora, Ill. for a meet
with Twin 9902, which had just come in from Chicago with
what *Railway Age* described as "44 sets of human twins . . .
selected by the Burlington from territory along its lines, ranging from 3 to 73 years of age." After suitable ceremonies, the
twins were split up between the two trains (fortunately, there
were apparently no Siamese twins living in CB&Q territory),
which then proceeded side by side over the three-track main
line into Chicago, 38 miles distant.

Next day twins Marion and Frances Beeler simultaneously broke champagne bottles over the silver noses of the Twin Zephyrs. Still more exhibition trips followed until, on April 21, Nos. 9901 and 9902 entered the public timetable, each making a one-way trip daily over the Chicago-St. Paul-Minneapolis route.

The Twins found both company and competition. As early as January 2, 1935, Chicago & North Western had jumped the speed gun by installing the "400" (so named because it ran approximately 400 miles in 400 minutes—technically, 408 miles in 390 minutes) between Chicago and St. Paul. The 400's were refurbished conventional cars, drawn by souped-up oil-burning Pacific-type steam engines, and their public reception served notice that other railroads would have to be on their mettle. On May 29, little more than a month after the Twin Zephyrs entered service, Milwaukee Road introduced the Hiawatha, a nonarticulated streamliner drawn by specially constructed streamlined steam engines.

75

All three competitors were booked between Chicago and St. Paul in 6½ hours, 1½ hours faster than the next best schedules of the day.

In their first week of revenue service the Twin Zephyrs averaged 86 passengers per trip for 97.7 per cent seat occupancy. Between runs, the streamliners ran supplemental round trips between Chicago and Aurora to acquaint the public with the diesel era, and these, too, were sold out weeks in advance. Finally on June 2, 1935, the railroad doubled Chicago-Twin Cities Zephyr service by scheduling a round trip daily for each of the Twins (*i.e.*, 882 miles per day per train!). During the months of June and July the consulting engineers of Coverdale & Colpitts reported that the Twins grossed $1.178 per train-mile vs. expenses of just $0.452.

Being revolutionary prototypes (as well as man-made machines), these pioneer Zephyr trains were not perfect. Fred Gurley, then CB&Q's Assistant Vice President and later President of the Santa Fe, said, "We had troubles with our gas-electric cars when we first received them. Our diesels have not been perfect, any more than other motive power." And he added dryly, "Periodical staff meetings are still held to discuss steam engine failures."

An official recalls that there were "proud moments among the supporters of steam locomotives when these engines pulled their trains into the terminal on time." For example, on July 5 and 6, 1935, a burned-out armature bearing put one of the Twins in the shop, so Burlington substituted a light Pacific type steam locomotive and four air-conditioned cars. On the runs to Minneapolis the streamliner's standby lost almost a half hour both days, but returning to Chicago the Pacifics soared along, once arriving only 6 minutes late despite four slow orders because of rain-softened track and an engine change at North La Crosse, Wis.

Yet the Zephyrs' 97 per cent availability record seldom permitted such exciting flashbacks to an era in which speed was necessarily synonymous with steam. The diesel trains suffered momentary setbacks from fuel-line air locks, generator "flashovers," roller bearing failures in traction motors, and similar mechanical troubles, but a maintenance staff previously conditioned to the new age by gas-electric cars solved the problems as they arose.

In the fall of 1935 the Burlington acquired its fourth streamliner, the four-car articulated Mark Twain Zephyr, No. 9903, and celebrated its delivery with yet another daring speed exploit. On October 23, the newest Zephyr, running minus its baggage car for test purposes and weighing 120 tons total, hurtled along recently relocated track in the Republican River Valley from McCook to Oxford, Nebr., at speeds well over 100 mph. Two days later the train, which bore a bronze bas-relief bust of its namesake as well as a reproduction of his signature on its observation car, was christened at Hannibal, Mo., by a granddaughter of Samuel Clemens. On October 28, No. 9903 began regular service between St. Louis and Burlington, Ia., making a 442-mile round trip each day.

77

Clearly the time was at hand for a truly long-distance streamliner, a train which would at one stroke combine the range of coach, Pullman, dining and lounge accommodations of a conventional limited such as the crack Aristocrat with the speed, cleanliness, comfort and modernity symbolized by the Zephyrs. Burlington was thinking of an overnight 16-hour schedule between Chicago and Denver, 1034 miles, and the question of whether steam or diesel power should be used—still not quite an academic issue in those days—was considered and answered.

Speed, for example. Steam engines were capable of running in excess of 100 mph. Indeed, if steam power was chosen, Burlington reasoned, such terrific bursts of speed would be mandatory wherever track conditions permitted in order to recover the time lost en route taking on water and coal, cleaning the fire, and being lubricated. A diesel, which could make a thousand miles without intermediate servicing, would be able to cruise at a lower, more comfortable average speed on the same schedule, yet still keep enough power in reserve for time recovery in case of delays. Again, the diesel would be easier on the track because its traction motors, being rotating machines, did not hammer the rail with the dynamic augment created by the side rods of the reciprocating steam engine. So far as relative fuel costs went, the point was decided by distance. In 1935 there were arguments that a dollar's worth of coal could do more work than a dollar's worth of relatively high-priced diesel fuel, but the 1034-mile run to Denver virtually demanded an oil-burning steam locomotive if an engine change en route was to be avoided. An oil-burner would avoid fuel and ash-handling delays which, in the case of a coal-fired engine, would warrant exchanging power for a freshly serviced steamer after the first 500 miles. Yet oil did a lot more work for the money in diesel cylinders than in a steam engine's firebox.

Finally, the railroad asked, which type of motive power would run the most miles per month and between repairs? A couple of handy case histories proved informative. At that time the original Zephyr, No. 9900, was making 500 miles a day; and out on the western end of the system a heavy S-4 class Hudson steam locomotive was covering 510 miles a day round trip between Denver and McCook, Nebr., powering the Aristocrat. The Zephyr had an availability record of 96.1 per cent vs. 69.2 per cent for the steamer. In other words, the Hudson was out of service more than a fourth of the time, the diesel less than one-twentieth of the time. In a 2½-year period the steam engine was given a general shopping three times, receiving a complete set of flues and a renewed back flue sheet on each occasion because of the pitting action of water used in that territory. The size and weight of moving parts on the diesel, though, made it possible to inspect and replace (if necessary) such components as pistons during normal layover periods. If a traction motor required attention, a spare power truck was placed under the streamliner so that the Zephyr could be back in service while the motor was under repair. In fact such was the availability of the Zephyrs in high-speed passenger service that the Burlington decided that its "experience definitely supports the conclusion that one steam engine is not the equal of one diesel-electric in productivity."

Thus it was that the Burlington placed orders in early 1936 for two 10-car Denver Zephyrs, both to be constructed of Shotwelded stainless steel by Budd and powered by Electro-Motive diesels. Less than a month later the railroad contracted for two new and larger Twin Zephyrs from the same suppliers. The significance of these announcements was that they signaled the end of the diesel streamliner's probation.

What had been an experiment in 1934 had become an accepted fact in early 1936. The new trains would have nonarticulated diesel locomotives with up to five times the horsepower of the original Zephyr; and in the case of the Denver equipment, their cars would feature cocktail lounges and dining rooms, as well as open berth and private-room sleeping accommodations.

While the new trains were abuilding, the original Zephyr, No. 9900, and the Mark Twain Zephyr, No. 9903, were installed on an overnight 16-hour Chicago-Denver schedule as the Advance Denver Zephyrs, to herald what was in the offing as well as to protect the road's mail contract. Buffet meals, free pillows, hostess service, and a remarkable on-time record quickly created for these trains a market far in excess of their limited seating capacity.

The new trains were well worth waiting for. Each of the Denver Zephyrs, Nos. 9906 and 9907, measured 883 feet 9 inches from diesels to observation. Motive power was supplied by an 1800 h.p. control unit, which contained a pair of two-cycle 900 h.p. V-12 engines, and a 1200 h.p. booster, which mounted a single V-16 diesel. The semiarticulated train behind included a mail-baggage car with auxiliary diesel-alternator sets for lighting and air-conditioning, a dormitory car with a cocktail lounge in one end, 2 coaches, a diner, 4 Pullmans, and a parlor-observation lounge. Revenue seating capacity totaled 102 coach seats, 93 berths, and 10 parlor chairs.

On October 23, 1936, No. 9906 was chosen by the railroad to even up an old score. On the occasion of the first Zephyr's astonishing Denver-to-Chicago dawn-to-dusk run, several railroad skeptics had dismissed the record by pointing out that the run had all been downhill "dropping from a mountain a mile high." In answer, a 3000 h.p. locomotive and six

A few of the dignitaries
aboard the Denver Zephyr for
the Chicago-Denver run
which, on October 23, 1936,
set the record for
the world's fastest
long-distance railroad run
LEFT TO RIGHT: *S. T. Bledsoe,
president of the Santa Fe;
Fred G. Gurley, assistant vice-
president of the Burlington;
Edward Flynn, executive vice-
president of the Burlington;
Gen. Chas. G. Dawes,
former vice-president
of the United States;
Ralph Budd, president
of the Burlington*
ON THE STEPS: *H. R. Clarke,
engineer maintenance-of-way
of the Burlington*
AT THROTTLE: *Jack Ford,
road foreman of engines
—Burlington*

cars nosed through a Western Union timing tape at Chicago
Union Station at precisely 7 a.m. and struck out through
snow flurries on a 1017.22 mile run west.

For almost three-fourths of the journey the spirits of those
aboard were often grayer than the low overhanging clouds
outside. At first there was wheel slip because of the icy rail;
then at Aurora, Ill., it was discovered that the 1200 h.p.
booster unit was delivering no power to the traction motors
despite its wide-open diesel because a mechanic had left the
reverser lever locked in a neutral position. West of Galesburg
there was a loud explosion and smoke poured out of the high-
voltage control cabinet in the lead unit because of a heavy

81

flashover, but fortunately the trouble was quickly remedied. Climbing West Burlington Hill, the locomotive's power output was suddenly reduced from 3000 to 2100 h.p. when an overspeed governor tripped, cutting back one of the 900 h.p. diesels to idling speed. Still later an air line broke (and was repaired with "a liberal amount of adhesive tape") and the air horns jammed (and thereafter had to be operated manually from the engineroom lest they reduce pressure to the extent that the brakes would have automatically applied).

Between "these disturbing interferences," as a Burlington official termed the mishaps with commendable restraint, the streamliner bored westward at a terrific pace, reeling off 26.6 straight miles in Illinois at an average speed of 105.8 mph, and touching 116 mph near Brush, Colo. The Denver Zephyr broke Western Union's timing tape in its namesake city at exactly 6:12 and 27 seconds p.m. (M.S.T.), having completed the run in 12 hours 12 minutes 27 seconds nonstop for an over-all average speed of 83.33 mph.

That was—and is—the world's fastest long-distance railroad run. Nothing else before or since, except the original Zephyr's exploit, has come even close.

The Denver Zephyr entered revenue service November 8, 1936, after being christened by Jane Garlow, a granddaughter of William F. (Buffalo Bill) Cody. She rode up to the train in Chicago on horseback and broke a bottle of champagne over its nose. On December 17 the two new seven-car Twin Zephyrs, Nos. 9904 and 9905, were christened when Minnesota Governor Petersen closed a switch in the state capitol to set up a radio tone beam which simultaneously released suspended bottles of champagne hanging over the new trains in Chicago Union Station and the Great Northern Station in Minneapolis. The Twins entered service next day, releasing No. 9901 for service between Fort Worth,

Dallas, and Houston as the Sam Houston Zephyr; and No. 9902 for St. Louis-Kansas City operation as the Ozark State Zephyr.

The fleet of eight Zephyrs was then responsible for 13.5 per cent of the railroad's passenger train mileage, running off 5900 miles a day, or 2,153,500 miles a year. And they met their schedules with 95.4 per cent availability, in summer as well as in some of the bitterest storms to ever visit Burlington territory in winter.

Still more Zephyrs were added to the timetable. The General Pershing Zephyr entered service on the St. Louis-Kansas City run April 30, 1939 (where it replaced one of the original Twins, which then went into Ft. Worth-Houston service). The Silver Streak Zephyr went to work on the Lincoln-Omaha-Kansas City run April 15, 1940 (where it replaced the original 9900, renamed the Pioneer Zephyr, which in turn went to a St. Louis-Burlington, Ia. assignment). The

83

Texas Zephyrs went into operation between Denver and Dallas on August 23, 1940. And the Zephyr-Rocket, a joint Burlington-Rock Island operation, entered service between St. Louis and St. Paul-Minneapolis on January 7, 1941.

As its streamlined fleet expanded, the Burlington made two significant changes in the original Zephyr concept of 1934. First, the newer trains were formed of individual non-articulated cars which could be easily cut in and out of consists as traffic and repairs dictated. The fixed-train principle of articulation had saved on weight but had proved inflexible in operation. Second, the railroad began buying its diesel locomotives "off the shelf" from Electro-Motive, accepting standardized 2000 h.p. control and booster units instead of the customized "shovel nose" motive power which had first characterized Zephyr operation.

The worth of such diesels was reviewed by Superintendent of Automotive Equipment E. F. Weber when he said in 1943 that "formerly this type of power was always purchased as part of a special train, but these 4000 h.p. (two unit) diesels were purchased as just so much motive power to supplant their predecessors—the steam locomotives. A short time ago one of these diesels, pulling the Fast Mail consisting of 17 conventional cars, picked up 25 minutes from the schedule between Galesburg and Aurora, a distance of 124 miles. Such a feat would be difficult to perform with any other type of motive power on the rails today."

It was also Weber who said this about the Zephyr age: "On some occasion almost everyone has had the opportunity of witnessing a modern streamlined train in action. If you happened to see a Zephyr, you first would notice a speck of stainless steel emerging out of the distant haze. Then in spectacular fashion it would flash by, a mass of shimmering steel, traveling a hundred miles an hour, and then within a course of seconds, vanish again into the distance."

And he added this tribute to the rapidity of the streamliner's debut and success:

"These sights are so commonplace today that little thought is given to the short span of time that has elapsed in the evolution of this class of rail transportation."

it Began with No. 103

"FOR GREAT DISTANCES during this trip, our speed exceeded 60 miles per hour and, while we rode in the quiet cab of this locomotive, we could not refrain from marveling at the apparent ease with which such enormous power was being developed. Here was a real challenge in a new field of service."

The year was 1940, the observer Burlington's E. F. Weber, and the locomotive No. 103. The 103 was a diesel, the property of General Motors' Electro-Motive Division, but a diesel such as neither the Burlington nor any other railroad had ever operated before. For strung out behind the 103 were 109 loaded freight cars grossing 6756 tons—and this different breed of diesel highballed that tonnage from Galesburg, Ill., to Chicago, 156 miles, in 3 hours 57½ minutes, including one stop, for an average speed of 39.23 miles per hour. Between December 11 and 20, 1940, No. 103 ran off 3929 miles on the Burlington, making two round trips from Chicago to Kansas City and one to Denver. That 10-day test constituted the handwriting on the wall. Thereafter the steam locomotive's days were numbered.

As early as 1938, a scant four years from the time when mechanics at the Budd plant in Philadelphia had spent four days just trying to crank up the Pioneer Zephyr's diesel engine, the Burlington was declaring that its "diesel-powered trains have proved so satisfactory in high-speed passenger service that ultimately all passenger trains will be propelled by diesel engines."

The diesel had also ventured into freight yards, and the Burlington, a bit self-consciously, had been buying such units "off the shelf." President Ralph Budd explained. "It is something entirely new," he said, "for a railroad to be able to order a half dozen switch engines and have them delivered within a week, just as one might purchase so many highway trucks, but that has been our experience and the experience of other roads since the Electro-Motive plant has been going at La Grange. A unique feature of operations in our Western Avenue Yard at Chicago is that with normal business, the entire Yard is handled with a fleet of diesels. Incidental costs such as maintenance of roundhouse, turntable, water, and fuel station facilities are entirely avoided. . . . These switchers work practically continuously, and I mean that literally. They have to take water and fuel only once in four days."

But despite the hurtling Zephyrs and round-the-clock yard diesels, the steam locomotive remained the unchallenged monarch of the Burlington, indeed of the entire industry. Ralph Budd observed, "Switching units represent about one-fifth of the 45,000 locomotives on American railways, passenger units another fifth; the other three-fifths are road freight locomotives. In the last mentioned class I have no actual experience with diesels to relate. Except for some transfers between terminals located a few miles apart, line haul has been performed with steam locomotives."

Many thought that it would always be. Experts argued with graph and formula in the trade press that the expensive diesel could justify itself only in terminal use. Public acclaim over the diesel streamliners had been dismissed by one locomotive builder as "ballyhoo," and it was widely predicted that steam would overcome diesel power just as it had withstood the threat of the straight electric locomotive. As for a freight diesel, the opinion of another builder was this: "Simply inconceivable."

But even as the steam locomotive was praised, its undoing was in the lab. From the beginning, General Motors had been less than completely satisfied with the original 201-model two-cycle diesel engine installed in the Pioneer Zephyr and its offspring. The 201 had not been specifically designed for railroad service; it wasn't adapted to mass production; and its three versions—an inline 8, a V-12, and a V-16—did not have wholly interchangeable components and lacked accessibility for maintenance. So in 1937 "Boss" Kettering and his team went to work on a new, more powerful, completely standardized line of engines for locomotive use. The resultant 567 series—a 600 h.p. V-6, a 1000 h.p. V-12, and a 1350 h.p. V-16—had one cylinder size in common, interchangeable components, and an easy-to-get-at layout. The first of them rolled off the new production line of GM's Electro-Motive plant in La Grange, Ill., in 1938.

The 567-series engine which intrigued the locomotive design engineers was the V-16. Bear in mind that the standard passenger unit produced by Electro-Motive in 1938 was a 2000 h.p. job which contained a pair of 1000 h.p. V-12 engines. It rode on a pair of six-wheel trucks, but only four of its six axles were powered; the others were idlers for improved riding at extremely high speed. Why not, reasoned the engineers, build a shorter unit containing a single engine—the 1350 h.p. V-16—and mount it on a couple of four-wheel trucks, with all axles powered and traction motors geared

down for maximum starting power but lower top speed? Four such units, coupled together and operated by one crew under multiple-unit electric control circuits, would form a 5400 h.p. locomotive. For flexibility, a cab or control unit would be semi-permanently coupled to a booster unit to form a 2700 h.p. team equal to any average steam engine; or this combination would be coupled back to back with two similar units to create the 5400 h.p. machine which, having a control compartment at each end, wouldn't require a turntable. Such a four-unit diesel would weigh 912,000 pounds, have an over-all length of 193 feet, carry enough fuel (4800 gallons) for a 500-mile trip, run up to 75 miles per hour, and—if the slide-rule technicians were correct—produce approximately twice the starting power of the biggest steamer on rails.

And early in November, 1939 all the equations and blueprints became reality. Numbered 103, the experimental freight diesel dressed in dark green with yellow striping slipped quietly out of La Grange, Ill., for a brief shakedown on B&O, returned to Electro-Motive for adjustments, then left again on November 25 to challenge the fiercest steam competitors the railroads could nominate. In the next 11 months, No. 103 rolled 83,764 miles on 20 railroads in 35 states, operating at altitudes ranging from sea level to 10,240 feet and through temperatures from 40 degrees below zero to 115 above. Not a single delay was charged to 103 en route; regular steam enginemen, under the supervision of Electro-Motive technicians, handled the demonstrator throughout its tour. Its performance was superlative. Out in California on 25 miles of heavy 2.55 per cent grade up to the famous Tehachapi Loop, the biggest articulated steam engines took 1350 tons uphill in 2 hours 15 minutes; No. 103 took 1800 tons in 1½ hours. Over a roller-coaster grade through Ohio

into Pennsylvania the diesel took 5000 tons; the steam rating was 2800 tons. And nationwide, the diesel's fuel costs averaged 6.7 cents per 1000 gross ton-miles vs. 13.7 cents for the steam power with which it competed.

This was the diesel whose effortless mile-a-minute pace with 109 cars so amazed Burlington observer E. F. Weber in December, 1940. He spoke glowingly of its "extremely high tractive effort" (228,000 pounds vs. 83,300 pounds for the Burlington's largest steam freight engine) —a power so great that 103, in inexperienced hands, broke six coupler knuckles and four drawbars when starting Burlington trains. And

Weber marveled at the fact that "it was quite difficult to slip the wheels."

Burlington did not immediately order such freight diesels from Electro-Motive. For one thing, the railroad had just built 15 additional 4-8-4 type steam locomotives at its West Burlington Shops in 1938 and 1940, and though these O-5 class engines could double as passenger power they were primarily fast freighters. Moreover, the Burlington possessed abundant low-cost on-line coal supplies as well as moderately graded territory. Thus, while the railroad was impressed by the visit of Electro-Motive No. 103, it had no pressing need in 1940 to abandon steam freight power or to buy new locomotives of any type.

The war changed everything, of course. In 1940 the Burlington moved 31 million tons; in 1942 traffic had climbed to more than 49 million tons; and in 1944 the tide rose to 57 million tons. Simply by adding more cars to trains up to the capacity of the engine, any railroad has a greater reserve capacity than other modes of transport; and so it was on the Burlington. Whereas the average revenue freight-train load had been 657 tons in 1940, it was up to 1115 tons in 1944. Quicker turnarounds at terminals squeezed more miles per day out of every engine, too; and older locomotives, some even tabbed for scrap, were withdrawn from storage, shopped and reassigned to active duty. Thus, as America armed for and began to fight a world war on the far sides of two oceans, the railroads, including the Burlington, kept the pace. Still, by 1943 management deemed it imperative to acquire new locomotives; and the War Production Board, which allocated all such orders throughout the emergency, agreed.

In early 1944 Electro-Motive began delivering a fleet of 16 four-unit 5400 h.p. diesel freight locomotives which, though painted red and white, were in essence duplicates of

the pioneer 103 which had toured the railroads four years before. They did incorporate one invaluable refinement: dynamic braking. This development in control circuitry permitted the engineer to turn the electric traction motors into generators, in effect, on long downgrades; the power thus generated was dissipated through toasterlike grids in the roof

93

of the locomotive. The retarding effect of dynamic braking took much of the load off the train's air brake system and thereby lengthened brake shoe life as well as reducing thermal damage to car wheel treads.

The new diesels (or "motors," as they were termed when new, to differentiate them from steam locomotives in train orders and reports) quickly proved their worth by releasing more than 50 steam engines for service elsewhere on the war-strained system. Reams of statistics verified the drastic change they wrought. For example, on a moderate 0.66 per cent grade an O-5 4-8-4 was rated at 2555 tons at an average speed of 20 miles per hour, and the even larger M-4 2-10-4 could take 2780 tons at that pace. Yet a 5400-horsepower diesel could haul 4500 tons. Another example: The steam engines the diesels replaced had needed 17 times as many cars to move the fuel they consumed. (The full implication of this simple figure is spelled out on page 99 of this study.)

Thus dawned the possibility, indeed the inevitability, of total dieselization. In 1944, in its Zephyrs and 5400-horsepower freighters and round-the-clock yard diesels, the Burlington for the first time possessed the means to eliminate all of the 948 steam engines then riding its rails. Such a step would involve, of course, a huge investment in diesel power, construction of diesel servicing centers, and mass retraining of enginemen as well as shop employees in the intricacies of dieselization. But the returns on such capital expenditures promised a new era in railroading for the Burlington. At one stroke the diesel would mean more than doubling the tractive effort of the largest freight engines on the property as well as the abolishing of water plugs, coaling towers, and ash pits (and the expense and delay they constituted). No more would a dispatcher have to take into account the steaming ability of a particular engine, the grade of coal in its tender, even the reputation of the engineer, before calculating a train's estimated time across a division.

The rapidity of the revolution astonished even its creators. The two-cycle diesel engine had first revved up on the Burlington in 1934 as the 8-cylinder, 600-horsepower power plant of a frankly experimental vestpocket-size 97½-ton streamliner; just a decade later two-cycle power—four V-16's strong—was yelling away in the innards of a 456-ton giant of nine times the strength of the little 9900. The ballyhoo had turned into indisputable fact, the inconceivable had become reality.

The first of the big diesel freighters went to work in January, 1944. On April 10 its great-grandfather, the Pioneer Zephyr, eased up to the station in Lincoln, Nebr., to nudge an 8-foot steel knife which thereupon sliced through a birthday cake weighing more than 1000 pounds. Ten years old and 1,679,000 miles young, the Pioneer was toasted by some 600 guests—including Ralph Budd, Charles Kettering, and Edward G. Budd. If anyone had asked that day, these three gentlemen could have testified that it was possible—at least in railroading in 1944—to have your cake and eat it, too.

blueprint for Progress

IT IS AN AGONIZING EXPERIENCE for a peaceful and democratic society and its institutions to be thrust into the maw of all-out global war. And for the United States the readjustment to peacetime conditions after V-J Day was not without its difficulties. On page 15 of its 93rd annual report, the Burlington observed frankly that "conditions prevailing in 1946 made it impossible to provide freight and passenger service which was always fully adequate. ..."

The strain of war traffic abruptly eased and was just as quickly replaced by the fiercest of commercial competition. Passengers, for example. Throughout the war the Burlington had moved some 5 million military personnel. In 1945 alone the railroad had hauled 1.4 million troops; but in 1946 the number fell to just 611,615. At the same time, gasoline rationing was dropped, Detroit got back into auto production, and the airlines installed faster, four-engine equipment. Freight car shortages developed in the aftermath of many strikes (e.g., coal mines were shut down for 59 days in 1946) as industries sought to recover lost production time. And, in common with all railroads, the Burlington soon found itself squeezed into a vise of relatively static rates and spiraling costs.

The Burlington moved rapidly to shake off the weariness of war and bring itself up to full competitive strength. The drive toward dieselization was perhaps the most spectacular achievement of the postwar years. Diesels at once improved service and, by their economy, controlled the ravages of inflation. On December 31, 1946, the railroad owned 835 steam engines and 195 diesels; by the end of 1956 the count was 131 steamers and 659 diesel units. In the summer of 1947 the Burlington was running all through freight on its Chicago-Denver and Chicago-Twin Cities lines behind diesel power; virtually all of its named passenger trains, Zephyr and otherwise, were in diesel hands, too.

As the builder's art improved, unit horsepower steadily climbed. The original two-cycle V-type 16-cylinder engine rated at 1350 horsepower was so refined in the first postwar decade as to produce 1500 and then 1750 horsepower, yet neither its piston diameter of 8½ inches nor its stroke of 10 inches was altered and all major components remained interchangeable. Simultaneous improvements in V-12 engine design increased passenger locomotive unit horsepower from 2000 to 2250 to 2400. Moreover, as power output rose, so did part life. For example, when the Burlington installed its first 567-series diesel engines in 1938, Electro-Motive recommended replacement of pistons every 75,000 miles; after the war that mileage limit was raised to 750,000 miles, and records of pistons in service for more than a million miles were not uncommon.

From the start in 1934, Zephyr schedules had been diesel-powered and, therefore, fast. And once there were enough diesels in the freight pool, tonnage began to roll as never before. Chicago-Denver time, formerly 2½ to 3 days, was cut to 39 hours; Chicago-St. Paul freight movement was reduced from 23 to 15 hours. Some of the freight diesels began piling up 13,000 miles a month by virtue of holding down runs that took them to the extremities of the CB&Q map. For example, 6000-horsepower locomotives left Chicago on 15-day 6200-mile cycles that took them west to Denver, down into Texas (over subsidiaries Colorado & Southern and Fort Worth & Denver), thence up to Billings, Mont., and finally home to Chicago via Kansas City.

Each purchase of diesel power was the result of meticulous study which totaled up each minute of schedule time and every penny of operating expense the new locomotives could be expected to save. For example, in one recommendation for 15 5400-horsepower freight diesels and 15 1000-horsepower yard units, the analysts observed that 512 coal cars were required to move fuel for the steam locomotives which would be replaced, whereas only 30 tank cars would be necessary to haul oil for the diesels. Translated, these figures implied that the road would save 173,520 net car days per annum. Multiplied by earnings of $1 per car per day, this meant a saving of $173,520 a year on this item alone.

In a case involving the projected replacement of an O-5 class 4-8-4 steam engine by a 5400-horsepower freight diesel between Chicago (Cicero Yard) and Galesburg, Ill., researchers noted that on hotshot No. 67A the steamer would move 3200 tons on schedule whereas the diesel could take 4500 tons through in the same time; that while it would cost $107.22 to buy the steamer's coal, $53.88 to move it from the mine to lineside, and $4.32 to load it aboard the

99

tender, comparable charges for diesel fuel would be $192.69, $12.16, and 43 cents, respectively. Adjusting these figures for the increased tonnage moved by the diesel, the railroad would spend $26.72 less per trip to move the same amount of freight business behind the diesel, as compared with the steam engine.

Such painstaking, detailed cost accounting lay behind the purchase of each new diesel unit, for it wasn't enough for management to simply generalize about the speed and power and economy of the successor to steam; the diesel had to prove itself over and over again—down to the last decimal point.

The way of the diesels was smoothed by a fresh approach to signaling. From their infancy, railroad signals had been thought of as safety devices—that, and that alone. Their function was to prevent wrecks, particularly the head-on and rear-end collisions which once characterized single-track operation. One of the first roads to install automatic electric block signals, the Burlington first tried them in 1903, and had 2140 mainline miles so equipped by 1940. Yet such signals were robots designed only to protect. As a train passed a signal, the semaphore blade assumed a horizontal or "Stop" position—governed by impulses from track circuits set up by the passage of the train. Then, as the train passed signals beyond, the signal arm returned to a vertical or "Clear" indication.

But then came C.T.C.—centralized traffic control. Whereas the dispatcher formerly had run his division on the authority of timetable and train orders (relaying them by Morse code or phone to wayside station operators for delivery to trains), he could now expedite trains by push-button remote control. Like this: C.T.C. compresses into a foot-thick chest-high olive-drab metal cabinet control over

the switches at the end of all sidings used for train operation on a given district as well as control of the color-light signals which govern the movement of trains holding the main line or entering and leaving sidings at these points. A miniaturized track diagram of the district is reproduced on the cabinet just above the dispatcher's built-in desk. Tiny white lights on the panel indicate where the trains are; red and green lights reveal the position and indication of switches and signals, respectively.

As two trains approach each other on single track, the dispatcher decides which should take siding, then flips thumbsized levers on his panel and pushes a button. The engineer of the train taking siding finds a red-over-green signal indication and the siding switch open as his train approaches. The train enters the siding, the switch is closed, the other train proceeds past. In pre-C.T.C. days an allowance of 10 to 20 minutes would have had to be made every time a train entered a siding for the head brakeman and rear flagman to open and close the switches.

C.T.C., then, expedites as well as protects train movements. Indeed, it is so efficient as to give single track approximately 80 per cent of the train-handling capacity of double track. The Burlington had 200 route-miles of C.T.C. installed by 1940, added more during the war as the supply of such scarce materials as copper wire permitted, then moved swiftly after 1945 to complete the job. Today 1,492.97 miles of its system (1,651.17 actual track-miles) are remote-controlled by C.T.C., officially termed "train operation by signal indication without train orders."

CB&Q even has 124.62 miles of double- and triple-track main line under C.T.C. That is, in double-track territory both lines are signaled in both directions. Thus if a Zephyr moving 75 miles per hour overtakes a freight doing 50, the dispatcher simply "crosses him over" to the other main track through a remote-controlled switch (assuming no traffic moving the opposite direction is in the area, of course) and permits the streamliner to overtake the tonnage, then cross back over to run on ahead on the original route. Such advanced signaling has permitted the Burlington to double its traffic overnight on double-track lines when emergencies such as floods have obliged neighboring railroads to route their trains over the CB&Q; and it permits the three-track main line between Chicago and Aurora, 38 miles, to handle as many as 100 freight, passenger, and commuter trains in 24 hours, safely and without delay.

Today's Burlington dispatcher "talks" to trains in his district not only by signal indication but also by actual voice communication through the agency of radio. The railroad attempted such wireless contact as long ago as 1915, but the primitive equipment of that day rendered the experiment impractical. The advanced technology of World War II introduced very-high-frequency transmitters and receivers, so

Freight engineer, in diesel cab, talks by radio   with   *his conductor, a mile back in his caboose*

experimentation was resumed in 1943. Two years later a fixed station in Burlington's Chicago headquarters was successfully making contact with 22 yard engines in the area. In 1946 radio took to the road as cab-to-caboose or end-to-end communication equipment was installed aboard 11 diesel freight locomotives and 8 cabooses operating between Mc-Cook, Nebr., and Denver. Today wayside-to-train and end-to-end radio communication expedites freight-train movements over some 8000 miles of the Burlington; this vast network includes 53 fixed stations as well as equipment aboard 222 locomotives, 80 cabooses and other mobile units, plus 231 portable walkie-talkie sets. In addition, 85 yard engines are under radio surveillance.

Switchman, alongside train, gets orders   from   *engineer in switch engine*

If a conductor spots a hotbox from his caboose cupola, he simply picks up his radio-phone and calls the engineer 100 cars ahead; gone is the necessity to depend upon often-ineffective visual communication and to use the emergency brake valve in the caboose. Trains move in clear, instant verbal contact with each other and wayside stations, and between their own engines and cabooses.

But a railroad, no matter how durable or sophisticated its locomotives and communications and other appurtenances may be, remains at heart what its name implies—a road of rails from here to there. The engineer's ideal railroad— "straight as an arrow and flat as a pancake"—must needs remain an impossible objective because of the idiosyncrasies of geography. Yet an objective it must be because every degree of curvature or gradient reduces speed and tonnage as it increases fuel consumption. That is why the Burlington has never been "finished" except in the sense of physically connecting the cities on its map. In almost every annual report issued by the company one discovers "Road Improvements" being made in search of perfection—as a grade crossing separation project is begun here, a tight curve is eased out there, and yard tracks are rearranged for longer trains at yet another point. And in the minds of every engineering and operating officer, there exist plans for continuing improvements in the railroad.

As a case in point, consider the Burlington's route between Chicago and Kansas City. Burlington pioneered rail service between the two cities, introducing the first through trains in 1869 following the bridging of the Mississippi River at Quincy, Ill., and the Missouri River at Kansas City. By the end of the 19th century, though, six other railroads were providing such through service, and the Burlington began to lose competitively because of its longer, hillier route. The original line via Cameron Junction, Mo., was 478 miles for freight trains and 490 miles for passenger service, whereas competing lines were as short as 450 miles. Some 162 curves and ruling grades of 1.6 per cent held passenger and freight trains to schedules of 12 and 20 hours, respectively, in the 1940's. The answer was more than simply rebuilding. To place itself back in the Chicago-Kansas City business on a no-holds-barred basis, the Burlington had to build a brand-new high-speed railroad—from scratch.

Such a super railroad was projected on paper as long ago as 1902 and was revived during the depression by President Ralph Budd; financing difficulties postponed the new line on both occasions. Budd's enthusiasm could not be contained, however, and after World War II the Burlington's directors once more found the Kansas City Short-Cut on their agenda. This time approval was forthcoming, and in late November of 1949 the earth movers went to work. Many of them, appropriately enough, were powered by diesels—blood cousins of the engines in Zephyr and freight locomotives.

The short-cut involved completely rebuilding 28.2 miles of the Carrollton branch, beginning at a point 2.8 miles west of Brookfield, Mo. Beyond, the surveyors laid out markers for a wholly new 42.5-mile piece of railroad which would connect at Missouri City Junction with the Wabash, over which Burlington obtained trackage rights for 16 miles to Birmingham. Trains would again be on CB&Q rails for the final 12 miles from this town into Kansas City.

The project, begun in Budd's administration and completed under President H. C. Murphy, took 34 months and 16 million dollars. Big, yellow machines moved more than 9.3 million cubic yards of earth (including a cut through a hill 5500 feet long and 95 feet deep); meanwhile work crews came along to erect 44 bridges and install 496 culverts.

105

Whereas the old route had had 162 curves and 1.6 per cent grades, the new line possessed only 26 curves and no gradient steeper than 0.8 per cent. Fitted with 112-pound rail and centralized traffic control, the Kansas City Short-Cut—declared open October 28, 1952—was in every sense a "60-90" railroad—straight and flat enough to run freight trains a mile a minute and passenger trains up to 90 miles per hour—although modern Burlington practice holds Zephyrs well below that speed.

The Burlington promptly sliced its Chicago-Kansas City freight-train time by 6 hours, scheduling No. 77 overnight in 13½ hours. In early 1953, the road introduced two new Vista-Dome streamliners: the Kansas City Zephyr by day and the American Royal Zephyr by night.

Christening the Kansas City Zephyr and American Royal Zephyr, a local beauty queen does the honors in the traditional manner

"Red" Grange, who wore No. 77 as football's Galloping Ghost, christens hotshot freight No. 77, Burlington's Galloping Ghost operating over the new Kansas City Short-Cut

107

Even the most powerful of diesels and the straightest of routes cannot, of themselves, create fast freight service. It is inherent in railroad operation that freight cars must be classified several times en route from shipper to receiver. Any freight train is necessarily a collection of cars being forwarded from perhaps 100 points of origination to as many destinations; for a few hours they happen to be congregated in a single train which covers a leg of the intervening distance common to all.

Bear in mind that more than 60 per cent of the traffic which Burlington originates on its own lines is delivered to connecting railroads for ultimate delivery to off-line points (an example: dressed meat moving Omaha-Chicago, en route to New York City); and more than a third of all its traffic is received from connecting roads. Burlington reaches 22 major gateway cities and has more than 200 interchange points with other railroads. All of which means that freight cars must be continuously classified and reclassified. Unless this necessary classification is expedited with the most modern of tools, the resultant terminal delays can more than nullify the time-saving advantages of better locomotives and right of way.

There are essentially two ways to classify the cars of an arriving freight train at a gateway point. First and most common is flat switching. A yard engine couples onto one end of a cut of cars. Then, as the switch foreman relays signals to the engineer and a switchman uncouples the cars, the locomotive revs up, then stops; the uncoupled car rolls into its proper track assignment. The cut is pulled back past the switch and the process is repeated to drop the next car into its track. Each track holds cars for a different destination.

The second method is gravity switching. The cars are pushed up over a hump. At the apex, cars are uncoupled and roll downgrade through switches into their assigned tracks according to destination. In the original hump yards riders with brake clubs rode each car downgrade, winding up the manual brake wheel to slow the car to a safe speed for easy coupling with those already standing in the classification track below. Today, retarders—knifelike rail-mounted devices that grip the wheel flanges under compressed-air pressure—slow the cars. Because the hump yard eliminates the back-and-forth wasted motion of flat switching, it has become increasingly vital to modern freight-train classification.

The Burlington built its first modern hump classification yard equipped with retarders at Galesburg, Ill., in 1931 and added another hump there in 1942, then completed a third such facility in Lincoln, Nebr., in 1944. Its newest, finest automatic classification yard officially went into service in February, 1958 at Cicero, Ill., just 6.8 miles west of Chicago Union Station.

A bit of historical flashback will verify the adage that a railroad is never finished. The Burlington first purchased land for a freight yard on the Cicero site (it was called Hawthorne then) in 1880 and completed a yard there in 1889.

A new westbound yard was built at Cicero in 1899.

From 1906 to 1908 the yard site was elevated with fill.

As America entered World War I in 1917, a young engineer, destined to become president of the railroad—Harry C. Murphy—helped lay out an eastbound yard that was finished in 1918.

And another westbound yard was built in 1919.

Thereafter improvements in the physical layout of Cicero Yard were limited to track rearrangements, but diesel yard engines began replacing coal-burning six- and eight-wheel steam switchers before World War II; radio communications with yard enginemen were established in 1945; and an

109

ultra-modern merchandise freight handling station, House No. 9, was completed on the north side of the yard in 1955.

By that time Cicero Yard was outdated and ripe for renewal. It was really a series of small yards, bisected by the road's three-track Chicago-Aurora main line, and held together by little more than a common name. Yet Cicero was (and is) vitally important to the railroad and its customers. Cars for some 500 on-line industries in the Chicago area must be sorted there for traveling switch crews to pick up and deliver. Produce must be quickly cut out of arriving trains and sent over to the team tracks at Racine Avenue to meet guaranteed perishable schedules, and interchange loads and empties are being continuously exchanged with the jointly owned Belt Railway of Chicago's vast Clearing Yard.

In the early 1950's Burlington decided that the busiest end of the system needed a replacement for the old Cicero Yard—the most modern replacement which knowledgeable planning, earth-moving equipment, and electronic science could produce. First a delegation of officials toured the newest automatic hump yards in the East and South. Then they looked at other new yards in the Chicago area. Finally they cross-checked their findings with their own hump experience at Galesburg and Lincoln. Plans were drawn and a 20 x 4 foot scale model was built to speed construction and to instruct yard personnel.

Fundamental to the new Cicero yard was the relocation of the three-track main line around the north side of the facility so that through train movements—mainly Zephyrs and commuter trains—would not conflict with freight-car classification. Next, the yard, which in its revamped form had a length of 2.3 miles and covered 200 acres with 93 miles of track and attendant facilities, was realigned to comprise receiving and departure yards for both eastbound and westbound traffic, and—as its heart—a 43-track-wide 1240-car classification yard or "bowl." At the entrance to this bowl a hump was constructed some 16 feet above the lower end of the class tracks it was to feed.

Cicero, as rebuilt by 1958, can classify 5 cars a minute, 3000 a day. It works in this manner: Once the road diesels and caboose of an inbound freight train have been removed, the hump engine couples on the rear of its cars and begins to push them up to the hump. The cars pass over (1) a dragging-equipment detector, which automatically signals to the five-story hump tower any underside defects; (2) a device which detects broken wheel flanges—and so informs switch foreman, hump yardmaster, and switch engineman; and (3) a glass-enclosed below-track inspection pit, where car inspectors scrutinize brake rigging, flanges, axles, and other running gear. While the cars are undergoing this strenuous "physical," the tower operator is punching buttons to set up the switches which stretch down the side of the hump. His job is to tell his computer and controls to be ready to route two cars to classification track 43, for instance—and one to 16, and two to 23. In actual practice, he sets up three or four cuts in a group, and his electronic gear memorizes his instructions and stands ready to act.

Now the cars are at the crest of the hump, and a pin-puller, working on broadcast instructions from the switch foreman,

111

uncouples them into the cuts of one to three cars. As each car slips over the apex of the hump and starts to roll down the 4.36 per cent grade into the bowl, it is automatically weighed.

At this point in the classification process, automation takes over and performs two jobs. First, remembering the tower operator's instructions, the switch machine automatically and consecutively aligns each car's route through the switches to its final berth in the bowl. Second, the car's momentum down the hump and its ultimate coupling speed are automatically controlled. Each car's weight and speed are fed into an electronic computer, which "mixes" this information with the rolling resistance of curved and tangent track of the car's routing into the bowl, wind resistance on the hump and in the bowl, and the number of cars already standing in the assigned track (this determines exactly how far the car has to roll). The computer reaches a proper braking speed decision in less than one-thousandth of a second and transmits it to the retarders—which thereupon slow the car accordingly, holding the speed of the rolling car to within 1/10 m.p.h. of the speed desired at the end of its run down the slope and onto its classification track.

Cicero Yard cost the Burlington several million dollars and three years to construct; it effects operating economies sufficient to show a 10 per cent return on investment after taxes.

When the press saw the facility for the first time on February 27, 1958, President Murphy could not resist noting that Cicero "refutes the claim which we have all heard many times—that the railroads have been slow to adopt modern and improved equipment and techniques."

The typical Burlington passenger is unaware of Cicero Yard and its split-second technology, for the classification plant is but a blur of freight cars to the man or woman comfortably seated in a Zephyr speeding past at 60 miles per hour. The passenger's concern and interest naturally revolve about the streamliner—its speed, frequency, fare, and accommodations. And it is a matter of fact, not opinion, that no other railroad in America has exceeded, or perhaps even matched, the Burlington's ability to anticipate and to satisfy the public's demands in passenger service.

Just as the Burlington was first in 1934 with a diesel-powered streamliner, so it was first in 1945 with another spectacular equipment innovation: the Vista-Dome. The idea of roof-top visibility can be traced back to 1863 when a resourceful freight conductor erected a sort of skylight atop his caboose to maintain a better lookout on his train; his cupola became a standard fixture on cabooses across the country. In

115

1891 the *Scientific American* published an artist's concept for a passenger car that would afford its riders such high-level viewing of the scenery, and in 1902 the Canadian Pacific constructed a twin-cupola coach for the same purpose. The car and its sisters were retired in 1913 and passengers stayed under roof until, to be specific, July 23, 1945.

One day in 1944, General Motors executive C. R. Osborn chanced to be riding a freight diesel through the Rockies near Glenwood Springs, Colo., and the superb visibility in the mountains made him exclaim, "If people knew what they could see from here, they would pay $500 just to sit in the fireman's seat from Chicago to the Coast."

Osborn sketched out an idea for a passenger car with a glass-covered roof compartment on hotel stationery in Salt Lake City. GM's Electro-Motive Division checked out the engineering feasibility of such a car and forwarded the plan to the corporation's Styling Section in Detroit. There eventually sketches were worked up for an entire "Train of To-morrow" (which GM contracted for and sent on tour in 1947).

One of the railroad officials who saw GM's first sketches was Burlington's Ralph Budd. And being the imaginative man he was, Budd sent a directive to the road's Aurora Shops: Build a glass-covered upper deck into a streamlined coach. In June, 1945 that car, called Silver Dome, left the shops, and it made its first revenue trip out of Chicago to the Twin Cities on July 23.

Public response was immediate and affirmative. *Trains* Magazine was to define the dome as "a new dimension in travel" which provides the "odd sensation . . . that one is sitting almost on top of the engineer . . . It lends an impression of being outdoors at 60 miles per hour and provides (for the first time in any form of overland travel) a full sweep of vision: ahead, behind, on both sides, and straight up." Burlington rebuilt another coach into a Vista-Dome and then— before the year was out—placed orders with the Budd Company for new Chicago-Twin Cities and Chicago-California trains, each incorporating five Vista-Dome cars.

The new Twin Zephyrs, which entered service December 19, 1947, became the first Vista-Dome streamliners in the nation. Each train consisted of a club-lounge car, 4 coach

domes, a diner, and a dome observation-parlor car. In a sense, re-equipping the Twins was almost expected of the railroad by a public which had come to associate them with all that was modern about railroading. The original Twins of 1935 had gone into service when the road had been ticketing only 13 through passengers a day each way on its only daytime Chicago-Twin Cities train. The Twins had soon sold out their 88 seats apiece, so Burlington had been obliged to make a round-trip with each train daily—a practice surviving to this day. In 1936 the first Twins had been replaced with larger six-car streamliners and a seventh car had been added to each of these in 1937. For years on end the trains' speed had been dazzling, and they were destined to be the world's fastest passenger schedules in the 1950's. So it was only fitting that the first Vista-Dome car should be placed in a Twin Zephyr in 1945 and that the Twins should become the first domed streamliners two years later.

Yet, the Burlington had another, far more surprising, Vista-Dome ace up its sleeve. The railroad was ready to devote its considerable streamliner experience to a new market, developing for it an essentially fresh philosophy of train operation. In the works was a Zephyr designed to more than double the route-distance of the longest streamlined train service on the system, a Zephyr that would unite three railroads in a common effort.

The Burlington, together with Denver & Rio Grande Western and Western Pacific, was determined to exploit the roads' joint Chicago-San Francisco route of more than 2500 miles. Which was quite a decision. The CB&Q-D&RGW-WP hookup formed the nation's newest transcontinental. It had been made possible in 1934 by the completion of the Dotsero Cutoff on the Rio Grande, which in turn had enabled the Moffat Tunnel to be used in direct east-west service between Denver and Salt Lake City. Yet the newest of routes (and the least known to the travelers) was 300 miles longer than the oldest, the Overland. Until 1939 only a single through sleeping car on an 80-hour schedule had been provided for the few riders who knew of the longer way west.

The Golden Gate International Exposition of 1939-1940, staged on Treasure Island between San Francisco and Oakland, had encouraged CB&Q, D&RGW, and WP to sponsor a through train via the Moffat Tunnel to the coast on a schedule cut to 60 hours. The Exposition Flyer, as it was called, had standard equipment and mostly steam power, but it boasted air-conditioning and economy meals as cheap as 90 cents a day. And, as Flyer passengers discovered, the train traversed some of the most magnificent mountain scenery on any railroad on the continent. Its three proprietors made the train a year-round schedule and thereafter World War II traffic jammed its cars.

As the three railroads faced the postwar period, a long-term decision about the disposition of the Exposition Flyer became mandatory. Its equipment would have to be completely replaced with streamlined cars and diesels if the schedule were to survive the already streamlined Overland Route competition, to say nothing of expected traffic inroads

119

by the plane and automobile. Yet CB&Q-D&RGW-WP could not hope to match their rivals' speed because of their mileage handicap. All they really had to brag about, then, was scenery—a line through Colorado's Rockies and California's famous Feather River Canyon in the Sierra Nevada. Suppose, the three roads reasoned, they replaced the old Flyer with a daily Vista-Dome California Zephyr on a schedule purposely timed to traverse the most scenic miles during daylight hours; and suppose the new operation was operated (in the manner of an ocean liner) as a cruise train, with the emphasis placed upon having fun en route—what then? An affirmative answer meant investing approximately 15 million dollars in the 66 cars (nearly half of them Vista-Domes) and 20 diesel units to create six identical streamliners necessary to provide daily service between Chicago and the Bay area.

The Burlington, the Rio Grande and the Western Pacific, all agreed, ordered enough stainless-steel equipment from the Budd Company in 1945 to form six 11-car trains; each California Zephyr was to have a baggage car, 3 Vista-Dome coaches, a buffet-lounge-dormitory car with Vista-Dome, a diner, 2 sleeping cars, and an observation-lounge-sleeper with Vista-Dome. The most arresting fact about each train's interior configuration was that there were 245 salable berths and seats vs. 224 non-salable seats. Virtually half the space on each California Zephyr, therefore, was set aside for lounging and looking. Downstairs in each coach, for example, there were 46 reclining leg-rest seats, each reserved and assigned in advance, but up in the dome there were 24 seats for viewing, not for sale.

There was more: a trained hostess (known as a Zephyrette) aboard the train . . . a public-address system throughout the train . . . a reservation system for dinner (passengers to select

5, 6, or 7 o'clock "sittings," thus being assured of a table when they were ready to eat) . . . and, of course, all the mountain scenery the most alert eyes could absorb.

The California Zephyr entered revenue service March 20, 1949, and quickly became in fact what its advertising was to claim: America's most talked-about train. For this streamliner wasn't built simply to move one from Chicago to the West Coast. Trains—excellent ones, too—had been doing that for years. No, the spirit of the "CZ" was that it was enjoyable in itself. Passengers met and chatted (as well as looked and took pictures) in the domes, got into the habit of stopping by the buffet car for between-meal snacks or pre-dinner cocktails, and became enamored of mountain passages unmarred by billboards and filling stations.

More than a decade later, the California Zephyr remains the most unusual of all Zephyrs and in many hearts the most beloved. Nos. 17 and 18, as they're carded in the timetables of all three roads, cruise along rather than hurry. The dining-car crews of the three operating railroads vie with each other for excellence of menus. Even the veteran travelers in the Vista-Dome gasp a bit as the train eases through the car washers at Denver and Portola, Calif., and the stainless steel streamliner is sprayed, then soaped, and finally rubbed down —domes and all—with big rotating brushes. And long after dusk, when most of the passengers are bedded down for the night, you'll still find people sitting up in the darkened domes, watching the signals flick from green to red and being lulled into a deep contentment by the faint clickety-clack of rail joints as the Zephyr strides across a starry Utah desert or over snow-laden Nebraska farmlands.

In the summer, especially, it's best to book your space early on the California Zephyr, for its repeat customers have made it a train with a waiting list.

Zephyrs carry their clientele 500, 1000, and even 2500 miles without change, yet some of Burlington's most faithful riders—21,000 of them to be exact—ride the railroad an average of just 17.1 miles each way, five days a week. They're Chicagoland commuters, of course, and very smart commuters, too, for they ignore their automobiles in favor of the dependability and comfort of diesel-powered, air-conditioned trains. Many Chicago railroad commuters enjoy such equipment today, but it was a different matter only a few years ago. Therein lies another Burlington story. After World War II the 38-mile Chicago-Aurora commuter service of the Burlington, like that of most railroads, was operated with coal-burning steam locomotives and sturdy straw-seat, non-air-conditioned cars. Nor was there any economic incentive for railroads generally to upgrade such suburban services. Commuters, to the traffic man, constitute a short-haul, five-days-a-week, sub-standard-fare business. To the operating man, commuters mean the provision of multiple mainline tracks as well as many engines and cars, all of which work at capacity only 4 out of each 24 hours (during the morning and late afternoon rush hours) and are virtually idle the rest of the time, including week ends. Then, as today, it wasn't a case of trying to make money on commuters; it was simply a case of trying to break even—and Burlington, like all railroads, didn't.

Several alternatives faced management. The railroad could have petitioned to abandon the service on grounds that it was hopelessly uneconomic and sapped the financial strength of the company. Such a move, however logical, would have been politically difficult and, in any event, the Burlington did not consider it. The suburban service pre-dated 1900 and the road felt an obligation toward those who had purchased homes in the communities along its right of way because of

123

the convenience of its commuter trains. Next, the railroad could have attempted a substantial fare increase; certainly the postwar spiral of wages and other costs would have justified such a hike. Yet the Burlington deemed it psychologically inexpedient to raise prices without product improvement.

Instead, the railroad allocated 15 million dollars to dieselize, accelerate, and air-condition its suburban service, a decision without precedent in postwar railroading. Enough extra passenger road diesels were added to the mainline pool to permit suburban runs between Zephyr assignments; one by one, the Pacific-type steam locomotives were withdrawn and scrapped. Some 70 pieces of existing equipment were refurbished and air-conditioned. And, in August, 1950, the road took delivery of the first of a fleet of stainless-steel, air-conditioned, gallery-type cars from the Budd Company.

Now the gallery design, since adopted by other commuter roads, was a technical breakthrough in the problem of how to carry more people during rush hours without extending the length of trains beyond the capacity of station platforms. As early as 1932 the Long Island had tried semi-double deck cars with seats in tiers but the experiment was never repeated, particularly because of crowded center aisle conditions during boarding and unloading. The Burlington cars were big,

but purposefully so; they had a length over couplers of 85 feet and stood 15 feet 8 inches above the rail. Riders boarded through a depressed-stair center vestibule with pneumatically operated slide-type doors. Once aboard they took either double seats downstairs or single seats topside in upper "galleries" reached by curving stairways adjacent to the vestibule. A gallery car seats 148.

At one stroke the gallery car—very much a Burlington innovation in its final form—solved three problems for the railroad. First, the gallery allowed the road to substantially increase the capacity of its rush-hour commuter trains without running consists of such excessive lengths that they would not fit existing station platforms. Second, the galleries enabled the line to haul more commuters without a proportionate increase in its Chicago Union Station usage fees, which are figured on a per-car basis. Third, the Burlington could continue to store its commuter equipment at the 14th Street coach yard between rush hours; had conventional cars been acquired to handle the increasing commuter traffic, expanded storage facilities (not available at 14th Street) would have been needed for use during the lull between 9 a.m. and 4 p.m. And since this is the Burlington, of course the road hasn't been content to let well enough alone. On week ends the gallery cars are often pressed into excursion service on railfan extras, fall foliage jaunts, and the like.

Of all the thousands of commuters who've ridden Burlington's gallery cars—the road now has 60 of the twin-deckers—perhaps the most impressed were the first 25. When the initial press run of the first two gallery cars was scheduled for September 6, 1950, the road invited its 25 oldest commuters to join the demonstration trip. It developed that to be eligible to join this select group, one had to have been riding the CB&Q for 45 years or more. The youngest man in the party bought his first ticket in 1905; the oldest, Dr. John B. Palmer of Riverside, Ill., a dentist, had been aboard since 1887.

In the midst of the Burlington's transition from war to peace, and during the year the California Zephyr was inaugurated and the Kansas City Short-Cut was begun and the company celebrated its 100th anniversary, there occurred a significant personnel change. President Ralph Budd retired August 31, 1949. It would have been difficult to express in words what the railroad thought of the distinguished gentleman whom the industry at large had long since selected as its elder statesman. The resolution adopted by the board of directors tried not so much to eulogize the man as it did simply to recount his impact:

> Mr. Budd became President at a time of severe business depression and bankruptcy of many railroads. His confidence in the Burlington and the country, and his vision, courage, and wise leadership, guided the Company through the depression, the World War, and the aftermath of political and social unrest. He brought the Company to an outstanding position, in plant and equipment, in earning power, in financial strength and credit, and in relations with the public and other railroads.

The man who took over the president's chair, Harry C. Murphy, joined the Burlington in 1914, and, except for three years in the Army Air Corps as a pilot in World War I, has been with the road ever since, rising rapidly through its engineering and operating departments to become Operating Vice President in 1945. As a line officer, he had been instrumental in carrying out the road's strategic decision to replace conventional passenger trains with Zephyrs, to replace steam power with diesels, to convert automatic block signal protection to centralized traffic control, and to carve out a cutoff to Kansas City. A reporter wrote of him: "He's been called both modest and honest—and a man 'not prone to cast aspersions on others.' He loves music, owns four cameras, likes nonfiction, enjoys nothing better than entertaining the grandchildren at his home in Aurora." Indeed, Harry Murphy is unassuming to the point that few know he anticipated road diesels as early as the middle 1920's. Again, his zeal in making of the Burlington the most modern railroad plant possible almost hides the fact that he delights to watch and hear the big O-5 steam engine the road has retained for excursion use. Such was, and is, the man the directors made custodian of the heritage left by Mr. Budd.

SD24, 2400 h.p.
per unit — acquired
by the Burlington in 1959

FT, 1350 h.p. per
— first freight die
on the
Burlington,
acquired in 1944

F7, 1500 h.p. per unit
— acquired in 1950

SD7, 1500 h.p. per unit
— acquired in 1953

GP20 , 2000 h.p. per unit
— acquired in 1961

Switcher ,
1000 h.p. — acquired in
1941. (Burlington's
first diesel switchers
were acquired in 1934)

GP7, 1500 h.p.
— acquired in 1951

, 2400 h.p. per unit
— acquired in
1954-55.
(Basic power of
the Zephyr fleet)

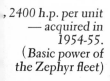

"A new high-level bridge over the Mississippi River at Quincy, Ill., was built at a cost of $9,750,000, and dedicated by President Harry C. Murphy on November 11, 1960, in a joint ceremony with the U. S. Army Corps of Engineers. The bridge replaces one built originally in 1868 and rebuilt during 1897-1902. It affords 300-foot horizontal and 63-foot vertical clearance."

— BURLINGTON ANNUAL REPORT, 1960

Chicago Area Freight House Eight.
A modern terminal, with over 350,000
square feet total covered area

NEW FREIGHT HOUSES IN CHICAG

Burlington's new Freight House
in North Kansas City, with over 100,000
square feet of space under one roof

D KANSAS CITY

Wide platforms along both sides
of four covered tracks expedite merchandise
handling for shippers and receivers
of freight moving to, from and
through Kansas City

dern facilities and strategic
tion (adjoining Burlington's new
ero Yard) make House Eight
eful transportation tool

overnight, Every night

THE FLAGSHIP of all Burlington streamliners, the Vista-Dome Denver Zephyr, arrives Chicago Union Station from Colorado as train No. 10 . . . at 9:15 a.m. The same equipment leaves in the afternoon as the westbound Denver Zephyr, train No. 1 . . . at 5 p.m. What makes the difference between Nos. 10 and 1 is the railroad's 14th Street coach yard. The long stainless-steel streamliner has barely ended its 1034-mile overnight run from the Rockies and passengers are still streaming up the platform when No. 9376, a 1000-horsepower diesel yard engine, grumbles up behind the observation car and locks couplers. The switch crew, one of 15 employed to handle the 700 passenger-train cars which 14th Street must turn, clean, inspect, restock and assemble into outgoing trains each 24 hours, must conserve the minutes today.

Today is the Wednesday before Thanksgiving, and 14th Street is acknowledging the reservations desks' holiday-size requests for seats and berths. Tonight's demand is extra-heavy, so No. 1 will be running west in two sections—a 14-car First No. 1 for Pullman passengers and a 14-car Second No. 1 for coach passengers. Both sections must be ready to leave for Union Station from the coach yard by 3:45 p.m. if the Denver Zephyr is to depart for the West by 5 p.m.

As soon as the last passenger has stepped off the inbound train, switcher No. 9376 goes to work. First, the streamliner is hauled backwards to Halsted Street, where it is turned on the wye track. Next, there's a brief stop at 14th Street to drop off a Slumbercoach which is booked out to Seattle on the North Coast Limited at 12:10 p.m. Then the train is pushed to the Morgan Street automatic car washer. Soap, water, and rotating brushes remove the dust of a thousand miles of high-speed travel. Finally, the yard engine pulls the train back into its berth at 14th Street.

The coach yard is ready. Car inspectors and airbrake men and pipe fitters and electricians close ranks on the Zephyr to inspect wheel flanges, disc brake shoes, generator driveshafts, thermostats, lights, steam-heat conduit gaskets, couplers and draft gear, truck springs and bolsters, air filters, heat valves—and a hundred other mechanical components. Meanwhile, inside the cars men are vacuuming rugs and upholstery (it takes a man 1½ hours per car to do the job) and girls are emptying ashtrays, dusting window ledges, changing head-rest covers, scrubbing out restrooms, replacing soap and hand towels and cups. The most time-consuming car is the diner. In the kitchen, floor racks must be removed and floors hosed. There are gas ranges to be scoured, grease and drip pans to be cleaned, stainless steel to be washed, dishwashers to be checked, propane gas tanks to be replenished. It's a 4 to 5 hour piece of work.

The cleaners are no sooner finished with the dining car than the steward and the chef go aboard to check and replenish supplies for this round trip to Denver: 105 pounds of prime ribs of beef, 40 9-ounce sirloin butt steaks, 15 pounds of smoked ham, 24 pounds of bacon, 45 dozen eggs, 7½ gallons of ice cream, 5 pounds of cooking salt. The long check list includes the little things: 126 packs saltines, 3 4½-ounce jars of olives, 10 individual buttermilks. And the staples: 20 heads of lettuce, 5 bunches of carrots, 30 pounds of granulated sugar. And, of course, the holiday fare: 30 pounds of turkey, 8 quarts of mincemeat, 24 baking apples. And we must not forget linen, silverware, glassware, and dishes: 96 water glasses, 108 teaspoons, 24 sugar bowls, 54 coffee cups and saucers, 5 jackets for each waiter, 50 54x61-inch tablecloths. The Zephyr's diner has served up to 200 per meal, and the culinary challenge thus posed may be gauged by the fact that the car has outside dimensions of 85 feet in length and 10 feet in width and that within these limits 3 cooks, 5 waiters, and a steward must serve a 48-seat dining room on a full-course menu out of a kitchen and pantry.

The relentless clock ticks past noon into the p.m. At 3:30 a pair of diesel road passenger locomotives (4000 horsepower) departs for the station; and 15 minutes later the two sections of No. 1 are dispatched out of 14th Street. First No. 1 will consist of a Railway Post Office, a baggage car, a dormitory car for the dining car crew, 2 Slumbercoaches, a diner, 7 Pullmans, and the Vista-Dome observation-lounge cars. Second No. 1 includes a mail car of magazines, 11 coaches, a diner, and a Vista-Dome buffet-lounge. A few minutes after four o'clock the two sections of the Denver Zephyr stand in Union Station on tracks 22 and 24—long stainless-steel lengths of bright windows and linen-draped tables and leg-rest seats and roomettes and bedrooms. Once again Burlington is ready to play host as well as to provide transportation.

The Denver Zephyrs are traditions as well as railroad

trains. They are excitingly different trains for first riders, a way of life for repeat customers. For less than 2½ cents a mile the coach passenger commands a leg-rest reclining seat with armrest ashtrays in a car with carpeted floors, individual reading lights, Venetian blinds and window drapes, porter service, and easy access to Vista-Domes. Or, for only a small space charge more, he can have single or double private rooms in the Slumbercoach, a new concept of overnight economy travel introduced by the Burlington when the Denver Zephyr was first unveiled. These compact rooms offer an armrest window seat by day and a bed by night—with private wash basin and toilet facilities.

The Pullmans are the newest in the land, and their room-

ette, bedroom, and compartment accommodations are possessed of all the extras. Roomette beds are of cutaway design so that they can be lowered without the need to open the door; compartments and bedrooms contain original paintings of native Colorado flowers, and adjoining rooms can be opened en suite for family travel or business conferences. For pre-dinner and afterhours relaxation there is the observation-lounge for Pullman passengers, with its Vista-Dome, rear lounge, and subdome Colorado Room (as well as 12 parlor chairs forward for short-haul first-class travelers). And for all passengers there is the midtrain Chuck Wagon car, a Vista-Dome buffet-lounge with lunch counter and coffee shop seating for beverages and snacks.

Newest of all Zephyrs, the present equipment entered service October 28, 1956, replacing the original 7½-million-mile Denver Zephyrs of 1936 (which merely required refurbishing to fit them for a new career between Denver and Dallas as the Texas Zephyrs). Additionally, through-car service to Colorado Springs, home of the new Air Force Academy, was established under an arrangement whereby a coach, sleeper, and Slumbercoach are forwarded beyond Denver on Rio Grande's streamlined Royal Gorge.

141

Burlington called its new "DZ's" of 1956 "big, full size, brand new," and they remain deserving of the accolade. One senses as much tonight, the eve of Thanksgiving, as No. 1 stands ready in two sections to receive the 650 travelers who've booked reservations for the West. And as the clocks of Union Station move toward five o'clock, they flock aboard: skiers in bright togs; businessmen heading home for the holiday; families off to see grandparents.

The wise ones, those sensitive to the intrigue of a great train's departure on a wintry evening, have found seats in a Vista-Dome when First No. 1 smoothly gets under way, slips from the embrace of the trainsheds into the signal-sparked throat of terminal tracks, and gathers momentum for the West. The line of stainless steel cars, glistening in the rain, rolls past the 14th Street coach yard, glides around the curve at Halsted Street and attains the straightaway. In the dome, a muted roar and the beams from two headlights, one fixed and the other rotating, are evidence of the 4000 diesel horsepower leading First No. 1 down the center track of the three-track main line out to suburban Aurora. The diesels bore through the wet night—past the overhead lights and endless freight cars at Cicero, on through the suburbia of Brookfield and La Grange. The Denver Zephyr overtakes a commuter train at Western Springs, then two more a few miles beyond.

And down below the darkened domes there is an end to the tension of office and city . . . and a beginning of relaxation. Couples, cards, and cocktails prevail in the Colorado Room. Ahead in the dining car the waiters fill water glasses, study the passengers' checks ("Let's see what we have here—shrimp cocktail, top sirloin, mashed potatoes, salad. Now, how would you like that steak, sir?"), and sing out orders to the cooks. It is all so routine, so serene, that even those who

142

concern themselves with such facts have to deliberately think about it to recall that the first Zephyr to Denver ran in 1936 and that before 1936 there was steam instead of diesel, Pullman-green cars instead of stainless-steel, and a journey that lasted from one noon to beyond the next instead of overnight.

143

It is good to be able to take for granted a travel institution such as the Denver Zephyr, to know that overnight every night it bridges a thousand miles between Lake Michigan and the Rockies with leg-rest seats and beds and dining rooms and lounges on wheels, to count on it from one generation to the next.

For it is a memorable experience to lie abed in a roomette with the Venetian blind raised and the dark, rainswept farmland outside sliding past at 75 miles per hour. Tonight there is the faint, compelling repetition of wheel clicks, the cushioned surge of speed—tomorrow morning there will be sunshine, Colorado carnations on the breakfast tables, the snow-mantled Rockies behind Denver.

Sleep comes easily within the security of such an institution as Burlington No. 1.

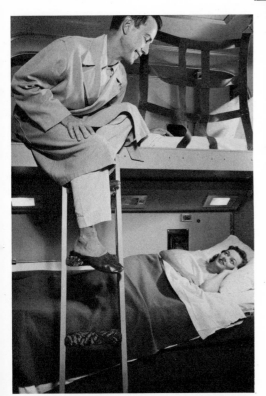

second generation Diesels

9 DIESELS WEST!

THEY CALL THEM GP30's and GP35's. They are the newest of railroad locomotives and, to a layman, bear not the remotest resemblance to the diesels which first began hauling Burlington freight trains in 1944. The World War II vintage unit, model FT, was streamlined; the newer locomotives definitely are not. The FT unit's normally aspirated V-16 engine was rated at 1350 horsepower; the GP30's turbocharged V-16 engine produces 2250 horsepower, and the GP35 turns up a potent 2500. The FT's electric traction motors had short-time ratings for maximum amperage conditions lest they overheat in low-speed drag service; the newer motors are self-protecting for all practical purposes, due to higher amperage ratings. The FT drew in engine-room air through filters which had to be removed and cleaned every 2000 miles or so; self-cleaning inertial type filters reduce maintenance of the GP30's and GP35's to a minimum.

These are second-generation diesels—power units to replace older diesels. To make economic sense, a new diesel must effect far greater savings than were necessary 20 years ago when this new kind of power replaced steam and rubbed out the costs of water towers, coaling facilities, ash pits, and so forth, in the process. Yet, when purchased to replace older diesels such as the FT, a GP30 or GP35 affords a railroad a bigger return on investment than did the FT when it first replaced steam engines. They save money in two basic areas. First, they pull more cars faster, so two new units can replace three older ones. Second, they require substantially less maintenance.

General Motors' Electro-Motive Division—the organization which powered the Burlington's railcars of the 1920's

147

2500 HP GENERAL PURPOSE LOCOMOTIV

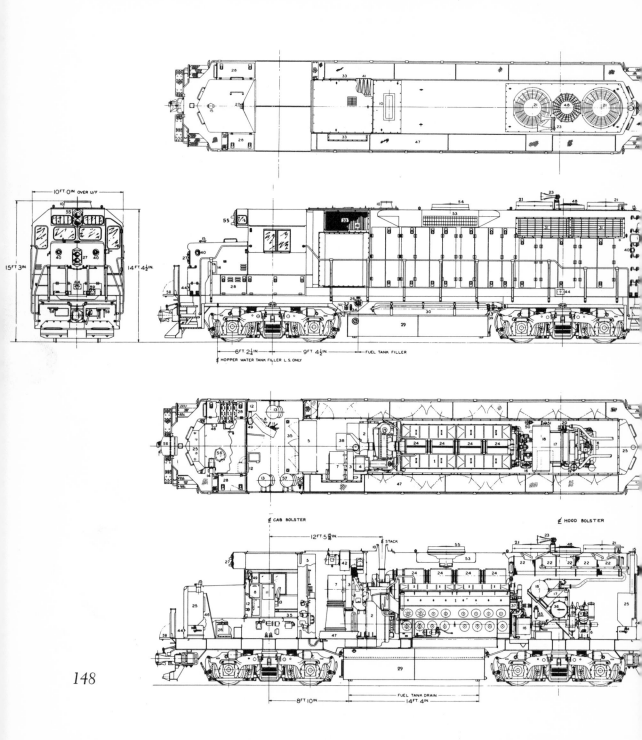

148

MODEL GP35

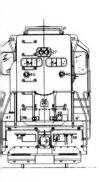

For drawings of 2250 H.P. Road Locomotive GP 30, see inside front cover

1. Engine — EMD Model 16-567 D3A
2. Main Generator And Alternator
3. Generator Blower
4. Auxiliary Generator — 10 KW
5. Control Cabinet
6. Air Compressor
7. Traction Motor Blower
8. Engineer's Control
9. Fuel Pump
10. Engine Exhaust Stack
11. Air Brake Valve
12. Cab Heater
13. Sliding Seat
14. Hand Brake
15. Sand Box Filler
16. Lube Oil Filler
17. Lube Oil Cooler
18. Engine Water Tank
19. Fuel Pressure Filter
20. Load Regulator
21. 48 Inch Fan And Motor
22. Radiator
23. Horns
24. Exhaust Manifold
25. Sand Box
26. Fuel Filler
27. Headlight — Twin Sealed Beam
28. Batteries
29. Fuel Tank — 2600 Gallons
30. Main Air Reservoir
31. Air Intake And Shutters
32. Emergency Fuel Cutoff
33. Engine Room Air Intake
34. Fuel Tank Gauge
35. Trap Door
36. Lube Oil Filter
37. Dual Fuel Filter
38. Engine Air Filter Unit
39. Automatic Drain Valve — No. 1 Reservoir
40. Classification Lights
41. Inertial Air Separator
42. Dust Evacuating Blower
43. Number Box
44. Walkway Light
45. Fuel Suction Filter
46. Collision Post
47. Traction Motor Air Duct
48. 36 Inch Fan And Motor
49. Speed Recorder
50. Fire Extinguisher
51. Engine Water Filler
52. Bell
53. Dynamic Brake
54. Dynamic Brake Fan
55. Signal Light
56. Toilet
57. Third Cab Seat
58. M.U. End Arrangement
59. M.U. Receptacle

149

and Pioneer Zephyr of 1934—introduced the GP30's in 1961. Typically, Burlington was among the first to place an order, just as it was in the spring of 1963, when the GP35's were first announced. There are many reasons for this rapport between Electro-Motive and Burlington, which extends back before the dawn of dieselization. There is standardization. For example, the bore and stroke of the cylinders in virtually all of the road's diesel engines are the same; inventory is simplified and reduced because the piston in a Chicago switcher is the exact twin of one in a freight hauler working out of Denver. Yet, in spite of standardization, there has been no corresponding freeze on product improvement, as the contrast in capacity between the FT and the newer diesels proves. And thanks to mass-production economies, the price which Burlington pays its builder for diesel power has remained pegged at approximately $90 per horsepower despite all the inroads of inflation.

For its part, Electro-Motive could ask for no finer showcase for its locomotives than the Burlington. The railroad's traffic and operations are sufficiently diversified to test the diesel locomotive's flexibility, and the road's longer hauls are capable of posting high engine utilization ratios. The Burlington diesels must move out of southern Illinois coal trains which gross as high as 10,000 tons (the weight of a World War II Liberty ship) concentrated between engine and caboose. . . . Assigned to a Chicago-Denver freight pool which forwards such hotshots as the 22¾-hour Advance CD, diesel units frequently average 20,000 miles or more per month, a figure which would have represented extraordinary passenger-locomotive mileage in the final years of steam power. . . . Across the system, freight diesels surmount grades which, in steam days, required six helper districts. . . . And

everywhere there are examples of diesels doing more than one type of work: the road engine which arrives in Edgemont, S. Dak., on a through freight in the morning spends the day switching the yard there before returning at night on another freight train; the road engine which arrives in Dayton's Bluff Yard at St. Paul on fast freight is uncoupled promptly and soon is moving across the Mississippi to Minneapolis with a transfer cut of cars to connecting lines.

In steam days each railroad ordered its own custom engines, and many were so tailored to the clearances and axle loadings of that railroad, and sometimes of even a single division, that few indeed were the instances when two connecting lines could pool their motive power to avoid engine

changes on interline movements. Today, of course, locomotives are standardized and purchased more or less "off the
shelf." This not only simplifies operations when a flood or
other emergency obliges a railroad to detour over its neigh-
bor's tracks, but makes it possible to interchange power on a
regular basis. On through hotshot freights jointly scheduled
by Burlington and Union Pacific through the Grand Island
(Nebr.) gateway the power is provided by 2250-horsepower
GP30's pooled by both roads; and these units, in multiples
of up to five and six units totaling 13,500 horsepower,
operate straight through from Chicago (Cicero Yard) to
Green River, Wyo. Another instance of efficient locomotive
use occurs when freight diesels of the Great Northern

153

operate east of the Twin Cities to Chicago. A similar example (in passenger service) sends Burlington units out of Chicago to the Twin Cities, and then over Great Northern rails to Havre, Mont.

Some grasp of the diesel's work capacity may be obtained from an examination of Pool DF-4, whose nine 4-unit 6000-horsepower freight locomotives operate on scheduled trains within a territory bounded by Chicago, Lincoln, Kansas City, St. Louis, and Peoria. A locomotive in Pool DF-4 sets forth from Chicago (Cicero Yard) at 7 p.m. Monday, for example, and returns home nine days later at 6 a.m., after operating 3044 miles and handling 17 different freights in the interim. The longer the haul, the greater the monthly mileage, of course. Pool DF-6, for example, provides for two 4-unit 6000-horsepower freight locomotives alternating between Lincoln, Nebr., and East St. Louis, Ill., 484 miles,

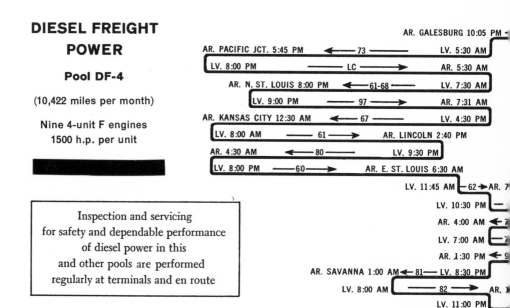

DIESEL FREIGHT POWER

Pool DF-4

(10,422 miles per month)

Nine 4-unit F engines
1500 h.p. per unit

Inspection and servicing
for safety and dependable performance
of diesel power in this
and other pools are performed
regularly at terminals and en route

AR. GALESBURG 10:05 PM

AR. PACIFIC JCT. 5:45 PM ◄—— 73 —— LV. 5:30 AM

LV. 8:00 PM —— LC ——► AR. 5:30 AM

AR. N. ST. LOUIS 8:00 PM ◄—61-68—— LV. 7:30 AM

LV. 9:00 PM —— 97 ——► AR. 7:31 AM

AR. KANSAS CITY 12:30 AM ◄—— 67 —— LV. 4:30 PM

LV. 8:00 AM —— 61 ——► AR. LINCOLN 2:40 PM

AR. 4:30 AM ◄—— 80 —— LV. 9:30 PM

LV. 8:00 PM ——60——► AR. E. ST. LOUIS 6:30 AM

LV. 11:45 AM —62—►AR. 7

LV. 10:30 PM

AR. 4:00 AM ◄—

LV. 7:00 AM

AR. 1:30 PM ◄—9

AR. SAVANNA 1:00 AM◄—81—— LV. 8:30 PM

LV. 8:00 AM —— 82 ——► AR.

LV. 11:00 PM

on trains 68 and 71. One of these diesels departs Lincoln at 7:15 a.m. Monday, say, on No. 68 and arrives East St. Louis at 8:30 p.m. that night; the engine is turned, refueled, and inspected, whereupon it departs on No. 71 at 11:30 p.m. and arrives Lincoln at 2 p.m. Tuesday. Freight locomotives in Pool DF-6 pile up 14,722 miles each per month, in a cycle which makes due allowance for scheduled maintenance and care.

Burlington's knack for diesel utilization came into national focus when the road managed to dieselize its 38-mile Chicago-Aurora suburban service without buying a single diesel for exclusive commuter assignments. Such exclusive assignments would have made it necessary to assign $180,000 units to an operation which works at maximum capacity only 4 hours out of 24 on a 5-day-week basis (i.e., two-hour morning and evening peak periods each weekday).

CHICAGO 7:00 PM

EORIA 1:00 AM

:45 AM

9:15 AM

1:00 AM

AR. 6:00 AM

	LEAVE					ARRIVE			
Terminal	Train	Time	Day	No.	Terminal	Time	Day	No.
Chicago	77	7:00 PM	Mon.	0	Galesburg	10:05 PM	Mon.	0
Galesburg	73	5:30 AM	Tues.	1	Pacific Jct.	5:45 PM	Tues.	1
Pacific Jct.	LC	8:00 PM	Tues.	1	Galesburg	5:30 AM	Wed.	2
Galesburg	61-68	7:30 AM	Wed.	2	N. St. Louis	8:00 PM	Wed.	2
N. St. Louis	97	9:00 PM	Wed.	2	Galesburg	7:31 AM	Thur.	3
Galesburg	67	4:30 PM	Thur.	3	Kansas City	12:30 AM	Fri.	4
Kansas City	61	8:00 AM	Fri.	4	Lincoln	2:40 PM	Fri.	4
Lincoln	80	9:30 PM	Fri.	4	Kansas City	4:30 AM	Sat.	5
Kansas City	60	8:00 PM	Sat.	5	E. St. Louis	6:30 AM	Sun.	6
E. St. Louis	62	11:45 AM	Sun.	6	Galesburg	7:45 PM	Sun.	6
Galesburg	68	10:30 PM	Sun.	6	Peoria	1:00 AM	Mon.	7
Peoria	75	1:45 AM	Mon.	7	Galesburg	4:00 AM	Mon.	7
Galesburg	70	7:00 AM	Mon.	7	Peoria	9:15 AM	Mon.	7
Peoria	91	11:00 AM	Mon.	7	Galesburg	1:30 PM	Mon.	7
Galesburg	81	8:30 PM	Mon.	7	Savanna	1:00 AM	Tues.	8
Savanna	82	8:00 AM	Tues.	8	Galesburg	1:00 PM	Tues.	8
Galesburg	78	11:00 PM	Tues.	8	Chicago	6:00 AM	Wed.	9

Instead of buying the 18 to 20 suburban diesels which would have been necessary to retire the older steam locomotives hauling commuters, Burlington's approach was to add a lesser number of conventional mainline 2250- and 2400-horsepower passenger diesels—and then to draw from its mainline passenger power pool to obtain engines for commuter trains. A dynamometer-car test bore out the railroad's hunch that the big E8 and E9 units could easily make the time on commuter trains without overheating their traction motors because of the start-and-stop nature of the schedules involved. And a maintenance program was evolved for the Aurora roundhouse, which houses suburban locomotives overnight between the evening and morning rushes. During layovers at Aurora, necessary attention is given to the diesels so that the units, upon their return to Chicago, will be available for outbound Zephyrs without further mechanical attention.

Here's an example of how the plan works: On November 10, 1961, diesel units 9965, 9967, and 9934A arrived from Denver with the California Zephyr at 2:05 p.m. That afternoon this multiple-unit locomotive was broken up into individual units. No. 9967 left Union Station with suburban train 165 for Aurora at 11:35 p.m.; No. 9934A left for Denver on No. 7 at 11:45 p.m.; and No. 9965 departed for Aurora with owl commuter train No. 103 at 2:10 a.m.

During the stock season, Burlington squeezes additional use out of its passenger units by assigning some of them to fast livestock specials, trains whose weight and schedules make them ideal consists for the silvery speedsters.

Each successive day of dieselization is a reaffirmation of the railroad's wisdom of a generation ago when it sponsored the largest gas-electric railcar fleet on rails and gathered the experience from which stemmed the decision to buy the original Zephyr of 1934. In retrospect, the gasoline engines of 30 years ago and more were cumbersome, yet underweight in horsepower and vulnerable to fire and failure. Although adequate for branch-line service, they seemed at the time to constitute not the remotest threat to the huge Hudsons and Northerns which proudly rode the high iron. Yet in the doodlebugs there was the germ of a revolution, an overthrow of dependence upon cinder pits and water plugs and coaling towers and an introduction to train operation which was unaffected by variables of fuel, weather, and crew seniority.

The new era dawned in 1934 when the Pioneer Zephyr hurtled across the prairies from Denver to Chicago, covering more than a thousand miles between daybreak and sunset, doing what no other train had ever done since the invention of the flanged wheel. Today (and since its presentation May 26, 1960) this history-maker rests outside Chicago's Museum of Science and Industry. Perhaps appropriately, the Pioneer Zephyr stands on a length of track beside captured German submarine U-505 and adjacent to a huge Santa Fe 4-8-4 steam locomotive, No. 2903. The diesel engine first gained international prominence as a source of propulsion for underwater naval craft. And steam power moved American trains from their inception until the diesel was adapted, in lightweight high-speed form, for locomotive use.

Museum visitors might well ponder at length the little stainless-steel streamliner that now stands mute and motionless after a service life of more than a quarter-century, during which it traveled 3.2 million miles and carried more than a million passengers.

For this is the experiment that became an example.

the Essence of the Story:

Self-Help the Best Help

10 DIESELS WEST!

UPON THE OCCASION of its 100th anniversary, the Chicago, Burlington & Quincy Railroad took note of its longevity in a special preface to its 1949 annual report. It read in part as follows:

> From the beginning the Burlington was located, planned, built, and run by men who were confident that under our incentive system of private enterprise the vast agricultural, mining, and industrial resources of the West would be developed, and that the railroad would be an important factor therein. On these two ideas they risked their time and money and, as John M. Forbes stated, "The projectors only underrated the pecuniary results of their work." Throughout the century of its operations the Burlington has never defaulted on an obligation and, beginning in 1851, paid dividends on its capital stock every year except three when its Missouri lines were torn up during the Civil War. At the close of 1949 all of its bonds were selling above par.

> The Company has lived through great wars and depressions; strikes, riots and civil commotion; droughts, floods, fires, and other calamities. It always faced trouble with unfailing courage and self-reliance and with confidence and faith in the country. Burlington history reveals that railroading has been a hard and strenuous business, but one in which good character and reputation may be built upon an earnest purpose to deal fairly with the public, with patrons, with communities served, with other railroads, with employees, and with those whose savings are invested directly and indirectly in the property. Past experience furnishes a guide for the future.

All too often those who write of railroading dwell on the past at the expense of the present. Textbooks, in particular, have much to say about the 19th century expansionist years of the railroads, yet almost take them for granted today on grounds that they represent a stable, even static, public utility in our time. The fact of the matter is that no management of the

Burlingon, to cite a specific property, has been more hard pressed to maintain and advance the property than the one which holds office now, and none has revealed a greater resourcefulness in fulfilling these obligations.

President Harry C. Murphy has written in *Railway Age* that, "Federal, state, and local governments have largely neutralized the efficiency of American railroads." That is, every mile of the Burlington today is paralleled by transportation facilities—highways, airways and/or inland waterways—constructed and maintained by public money of which only a fraction is reimbursed by the trucks, planes, and barges which make commercial use of this plant.

The inequity of private vs. public transportation facilities is expressed in several ways. Instead of merely generalizing about the differences, Harry Murphy has spelled them out in dollars and cents by comparing the financial performance of his railroad with that of five profitable truck lines and five profitable barge lines in CB&Q territory as indicated by their 1958 reports to the Interstate Commerce Commission.

The results of this study, as published in *Railway Age*, indicated that out of each freight revenue dollar the Burlington paid 5.03 cents in property taxes, for example, as against 0.45 cent paid by the truck lines and 0.51 cent by the barge lines. The discrepancy stems from the fact that the railroad's competition largely conducts its business on publicly owned and hence nontaxable property. Because the railroad owns the property over which it runs its trains, CB&Q must maintain it; out of each revenue freight dollar the Burlington must allocate 12.65 cents for maintenance of way and structures although equivalent maintenance costs of truck lines (including license fees and fuel taxes) absorb only 7.25 cents out of each revenue dollar and of barge lines just 0.58 cent.

Harry Murphy, no man to plead for special favor when confronted with equal competition, likes to cite a case in point of the dilemma which confronts him. A few years ago the Army Engineers received approval to lengthen lock No. 19 on the Mississippi River at Keokuk, Ia., so that it could accommodate 1200-foot instead of 530-foot barge tows. The change was purely to expedite barge traffic and not for any recreation, hydro-electric, land reclamation, flood control, or other purpose. It was completed at a cost of $14,275,000 in public monies, for which the barge lines made no payment inasmuch as they do not pay any form of user-charges or taxes for the use of facilities. For that kind of capital the Burlington could have erected four modern hump-retarder yards, enough to classify and expedite virtually all of the 1.3 million revenue carloads which the railroad hauls each year. Moreover, the company would have had to raise such money from earnings after taxes (CB&Q had a net income of just 12.4 million dollars in 1960 and has seldom earned more than 25 million since World War II) and then pay taxes on the new terminals once they were completed—and maintain them out of private funds thereafter, of course.

A railroad, as a common carrier, is rigidly regulated by the Interstate Commerce Commission at the national level as well as by public service commissions in all of the states it serves. It cannot raise or lower its rates without regulatory approval. It is not allowed to engage in water or airline operation. On the one hand, the Burlington's average freight rates, 1.327 cents per ton-mile in 1960 vs. .974 cents in 1945, have seldom kept pace with increases in wages and material costs; on the other, rail rates have frequently been held up as an umbrella over the competition in specific cases where reductions were asked on grounds of inherent rail efficiency. Again, Burlington has been obliged by law to offer a primarily rail transportation service rather than a total transportation service. Not long after the depression the railroad applied for permission to operate helicopters in order to ferry passengers to mainline points to connect with the Denver Zephyr. The railroad's request was rejected, partly on grounds that wingless aircraft were not yet dependable enough; but after the war Burlington joined with other railroads in seeking permission to operate air services and this time was rebuffed purely on grounds that it was a surface carrier.

No other private enterprise in the nation, besides railroading, has been compelled to meet its responsibilities to the public as well as to its employees and owners against such odds. The essence of the story told in this book is that the Burlington has subscribed with all of its energies to President Murphy's maxim that "Self-help is generally the best help." As this volume recounts, the railroad completely replaced reciprocating steam locomotives with diesel-electric power in a technological revolution without precedent in overland transportation. Additionally, Burlington replaced conventional passenger trains with Zephyrs; married the virtues of rail and highway carriage in piggyback; expedited and made safer train movements with centralized traffic control, radio communication, automatic freight-car classification, even a new short-cut to Kansas City, and otherwise improved itself and its service without once missing a payroll, omitting a penny in tax payments, defaulting on a debt, passing a dividend, or accepting a public subsidy.

The things set forth in this volume are a matter of record. But I have also observed Burlington men and their works firsthand. I took my first ride on the CB&Q almost 20 years ago, on a gas-electric car from Streator, Ill., up to Aurora, and since then too many miles to count have clicked off . . . on a hotshot freight riding the Kansas City Short-cut, on No. 42 as it bored through a ferocious Nebraska thunderstorm near Alliance, in cabs of diesels drumming along at 90 per up the banks of the Mississippi. I have walked the aisles of the road's shops at West Burlington and Aurora and watched endless freight cars humped at Lincoln and Galesburg and sat at the dispatcher's elbow before the C.T.C. board in McCook, Nebr., long after midnight.

And even more revealing, I have heard an Eastern railroad president, quite suspicious of routine publicity methods of image-building, declare that he wanted for his line "the reputation Ralph Budd built out of service for the Burlington."

Burlington! The very word has strength, good will, durability; for after all, what I found (and keep finding) in the railroad is but what Frank H. Spearman summed up in 1904 when he wrote in his *The Strategy of Great Railroads:*

> The story of the Burlington is in itself out of the ordinary. It has always been aggressive in its management and peculiarly successful in its ventures. Any Western railroad man esteems himself fortunate when he can get business away from the Burlington. To take a fall out of the Burlington is a feather in any railroad traffic manager's cap, and it is odds that for some time thereafter he will be kept busy in holding his ground, for, unless a very handy man, he is likely to be thrown on the defensive at once.
>
> This curiously strong grip on business has never been advanced by the cutting of rates, but rather by a keen realization

163

of the fact that business, like kissing, goes by favor. The Burlington management has always been characterized by astuteness, and its people have cultivated the art of making friends. Mr. Perkins, who made the wonderful road what it is, never liked to have enemies or trouble. His motto was, briefly, "80 per cent of the business, and peace;" and it is astonishing how closely he approximated his ideal. Somehow, too, the Burlington Road succeeded in creating among its men an *esprit de corps*, a loyalty to itself, so that former Burlington officials refer with pride to the old road. When one meets, East or West, on American roads a Burlington man he is conscious, too, of a consideration of the sort that asks, Now, what can I do for you? rather than, What can you do for me?

That was written more than half a century ago, in an age of railroad monopoly of transportation and years before other forms of transport known today were invented, much less developed to their present strength by Government assistance. Yet what Spearman grasped in the CB&Q of 1904 was the identical spirit that was to create the Zephyr, replace steam with diesel locomotives, and ask only equal treatment in regulation and taxation in our time.

This book is an excerpt from the continuing story of an "out-of-the-ordinary railroad," and, specifically, the tale of some ventures in which it was "peculiarly successful."